Do-It-Yourself
HEDGE FUNDS

Do-It-Yourself
HEDGE
FUNDS

Everything You Need to Make Millions Right Now

WAYNE P. WEDDINGTON III

BUSINESS PLUS

NEW YORK   BOSTON

Business Plus
Hachette Book Group
237 Park Avenue
New York, NY 10017 Visit our Web site at www.HachetteBookGroup.com.

Business Plus is an imprint of Grand Central Publishing. The Business Plus name and logo are trademarks of Hachette Book Group, Inc.

Printed in the United States of America

First Edition: January 2009

10 9 8 7 6 5 4 3 2 1

Library of Congress Cataloging-in-Publication Data

Weddington, Wayne P.
   Do-it-yourself hedge funds : everything you need to make millions right now / Wayne P. Weddington III.—1st ed.
      p. cm.
   Includes index.
   ISBN-13: 978-0-446-50389-1
   ISBN-10: 0-446-50389-4
   1. Hedge funds. 2. Investments. I. Title.

   HG4530.W39 2009
   332.64'524—dc22

                                          2008023558

Book design by Charles Sutherland

To my Mother who, to this day, lovingly believes that
I am a stockbroker.

To my Father, who had the beneficent wisdom to inform me,
only years later, that my leaving medical school
was the single most painful day of his life.

I love you.

AUTHOR'S NOTE

In the writing of this book, it was necessary on occasion to change the names and identifying characteristics of certain individuals. That being said, the basis of all the stories herein are true (as they say, you can't make this stuff up!).

In any event, please note that the names of Barry Bling-alot (Chapter 3); Moishe Lowenstein (Chapter 4); Joseph (Chapter 5); Jig Johnson (Chapter 6); the Global Macro Trader (Chapter 6); Karim (Chapter 8); and Joseph, Fernando, Adam, Stephen, Barry, and Michael (Chapter 10) have been changed.

CONTENTS

INTRODUCTION

I literally fell into finance. I had no idea what it was about. I knew that these business guys pranced around New York with briefcases and walked into glassy office buildings. I had once begun to read *Bonfire of the Vanities*, but I put it down because I could not stomach the extreme caricatures of New York personalities. I knew nothing.

I was a biochemistry major at Columbia University. I would say that I was a "cool" geek: I was pretty cool and somewhat popular, operating somewhere between Erkel and Billy Dee Williams.

In many ways I was lucky. My mother was a teacher, the career track that many ambitious, intelligent women took in the 1940s and 1950s. My father was a surgeon. So I was always around intellectual stimulation. It was always assumed that I would go into medicine. One could not tell me otherwise.

Science was what I knew and enjoyed. I did very well but not exceptionally well, mostly because I was easily distracted by my own imagination and the unyielding need to explore other curiosities.

It is probably a politically incorrect adage to say that behind every successful man is a woman. But such is how I started my career in finance. My girlfriend at the start of my career was Hanna, who had escaped to New York and to Barnard

College out of the eye of the Poland's Solidarnosc (Solidarity) storm. She was bright, driven, and loyal. She was also keenly aware of opportunity when it presented itself, and she was tired of me being a poor science student.

Hanna had become aware of a Wall Street internship program that had accepted the boyfriend of a girlfriend's girlfriend the previous summer. He had made $400 a week, which was an enormous sum of money for us at the time.

"You should apply," she would say. "What's wrong with you? How can it hurt? Just put in an application!"

Did I say I liked science? Perhaps I forgot to say that I was somewhat lazy, too. I probably had a litany of excuses, but I never got a "round tuit" to apply to the internship. Hanna, however, did not give up.

One night I was in my dorm room around midnight when the phone rang.

"What are you doing?" she asked.

"Oh, nothing," I whispered hoarsely.

"Great! Then you won't mind taking a pencil and writing out your personal experience on a piece of paper. It doesn't have to be neat; I can read your handwriting by now. And don't be lazy, I have the entire staff of the *Columbia Spectator* right here. They will stay the entire night with me until we finish typesetting your résumé and your application for this internship. I will be there in fifteen minutes to pick it up and you *better* have it done."

I dared not disappoint her, given she had gone to such lengths. Plus, she had this look of scathing disapproval that could curl your toes. It was very effective.

"Oh, and by the way, you need to write an essay about why you want to go into finance and why you are the best person for the job."

Still groggy, I set about putting pen to paper. I had no idea what I was talking about, let alone she. But I managed to scribble something down and write a little bit about myself. Right on time, Hanna arrived, with that disapproving smirk, to pick up the scribbled notes. As promised, she kept the staff of the *Spectator* at it until she had achieved the desired result: a beautifully rendered résumé and a narrative about myself that made it look and sound as if it would be foolhardy not to consider me. I was blessed to be loved, but I was too young to know it.

So that my application would have no exposure to my incapacity for timeliness, Hanna did everything. She organized it, packaged it, and licked the stamps. Off it went. Somewhere.

Would you believe it? I got an interview. I have no idea how. I grudgingly confessed to Hanna that yes, I was excited. Those who had gone through the interview process before warned me to be prepared for a long grilling conducted by three sadists. A couple of guys told me that they had been on the verge of tears. The interviewers could ask me about anything and would do so in rapid fire. What was worse, I had to somehow convince them that I was really interested in the job.

The interview would require a bit of "equipment" preparation, as well. I did not own a suit, nor did I own a proper business shirt or shoes. At the time, I was a student-worker in the food service at school to make sufficient money to pay for my tuition and books. Hanna helped me out by punching me in for phantom shifts on the job. She was also a work-study student and, fortunately for me, she was the manager of the food service. Eventually I had enough to buy a suit, shirt, and shoes for what would turn out to be the most important interview of my life. Yes, I probably could have asked my parents for help, but being an independent lad, that option never really occurred to me.

I went to purchase my interview clothes at a place called

Dollar Bills, which was a New York institution at the time for men and women who wanted to buy designer labels cheaply. It was located on Forty-second Street, in the bowels of Grand Central Terminal. "Jobber" was the term for Dollar Bills and stores of its kind, which would buy the aging or stale inventory of the high-end New York retailers for cents on the dollar, then sell it to their customers at steep discounts to the original retail price. Dollar Bills agreed not to advertise, so as not to cannibalize the high-end stores' sales. It was a real New York insiders' institution, especially for parsimonious shoppers like myself. I was able to buy a suit for very little money without looking cheesy. (Asian manufacturing and the Internet have since put jobbers out of business.)

Well, I bought a gray suit, black shoes, and a white shirt. I was ready. On the night before interview day, I laid them out neatly and set a few alarms to make sure that I woke up on time. I had had an incident earlier in the year where I managed to sleep through the alarm for my MCATs . . . but that's another story. (I was permitted to take the MCATs the next day, together with those who were observing the Shabbat on the regular test day, Saturday.)

The next morning, I donned my clothes and had all but forgotten about a necktie! No matter; I remembered that I had a tie in my wardrobe that would do just fine. It was woolen, burgundy, and about one-quarter inch wide . . . but its tragic qualities were lost on me. I managed to maneuver the necktie into a knot. It looked more like a shoelace than a necktie. I grabbed a briefcase (which was a mere prop, as there was nothing in it), and off I went.

Before I left my dorm, one of my suitemates—the dark evil one of us; there is one in every group—asked me why I was dressed up. I told him that I was off to an interview. I tried to hurry away, no doubt because I didn't want to be jinxed by his evil energy. He laughed at me. "You can't go to an interview looking like that. Dude, let me give you a tie."

Sherif took me into his room (the first time ever) and opened what appeared to be an armoire (yes, he had an armoire in a student dorm room) with a rack full of ties. I had never known that people my age were supposed to have those things. He handed me a blue Oscar de la Renta tie with Oscar's name neatly scripted, in small letters, diagonally across the bottom left side. It was the first act of kindness I had ever experienced from Sherif, and I was grateful.

The interview went well. As promised, three interviewers simultaneously grilled me. One of the interviewers was particularly skeptical about my desire to work on Wall Street. He twisted his mouth, sighed disparagingly, and shot me sidelong glances. The truth is there wasn't a *shred* of evidence that I had any interest in finance. I had no work experience or courses in economics. I had been smart enough to read the second and third columns of the *Wall Street Journal* daily for the prior three weeks, but other than that, I really knew nothing about business. The skeptical one wondered why the heck was I there. And he wondered aloud whether it would be better to groom someone who was more devoted to the field. I soldiered on. I finished the interview by saying something like, "When I am asked to do a job, I am thorough, meticulous, and complete. If you asked me to sweep the floor, I would not stop until I had removed every speck of dirt."

Whatever I said must have been effective. I got the job.

When I arrived to work at the investment bank, it was a whole new world to me. One of the things that I had to get used to was how well dressed everyone was. Everyone looked as if they were wearing their Sunday best . . . every day! You might recall that I had only one suit, so this was something of a bind for me. Let's just say that that suit got a *lot* of use, and

I put my hands on whatever suits or suit jackets I could find until I had a decent wardrobe.

One of the first notions of which I was disabused was that I would find offices rife with financial geniuses. There were egos, yes, but none of the high-minded brilliance that I had expected. Mind you, I am not saying that the people were stupid, but I was, after all, a biochemistry major. The only difference between me and the best, as far as I could tell, was exposure.

Another thing I had to adjust to was scale. Every project I worked on was a huge, multimillion-dollar deal. In the ordinary course of life, one simply did not add six, seven, or eight zeros when describing a financial transaction. I was barely comfortable discussing thousands, but every written piece of pro forma analysis was in the millions.

There were definitely raging egos at the bank, and to me that was the most perplexing of all. At that time the source of capital for the investment banks was primarily institutions. This was a time before the disintermediation that investors enjoy today. Today, if you want to make a trade you can open a brokerage account online and be trading in days, if not hours. Back then, you really needed a stockbroker to gain access to the markets. And you had to have enough money to be sure that the broker thought you were worth his time (in other words, whether he could charge you sufficiently and profitably).

Therefore, much of the money that facilitated investment banking activity was institutional money. It struck me as ironic that many of the top bankers, those who had reached "masters of the universe" status, were actually there indirectly through managing pensions, the money of common people. For example, my mother's pension adviser, TIAA-CREF, was an investor in many of the deals we did. Maybe that meant she indirectly invested a penny of each of those deals—probably less—but it was still her money, as well as the earnings of thousands of other teachers and municipal workers. We were basically investing the money of common people—people whom some of my fellow workers might disdain—and getting rich off it. I also saw that while it was the people's money, only a precious few—the bankers—really enjoyed the fruits in scale. In economics, I believe that's called the "paradox of value."

This is not to cast aspersion on those who work in the financial services industry, nor on the industry itself. As far as my experience goes, the industry has a very high density of bright and driven people. It is what has made my time on the Street the most enjoyable. The assholes-per-capita in finance was higher than in most professions, but the competition and the general level of competence was refreshing and inspiring. But they were not superhuman, which inspired me as well. "There are a whole lot of people here who make a *lot* of money who aren't brighter than I am," I would periodically say to myself to bolster my own sense of professional entitlement.

And this is what I want to convey to you, the reader. If you are reading this book, it is because you want something that has eluded you in the past. Maybe at some point you have taken over your own finances with a less-than-favorable result. Perhaps you have paid fees to a financial professional who provided less-than-anticipated results. Perhaps you have read about the magical performance of a hedge fund only to learn that you could not participate. Perhaps you simply want to sit at the same table so you can achieve some of the same gains and profits that the guys you read about do. The reality of high finance and investing probably seems so far away that it appears unachievable. But that, as I will show you, is not the case.

I do not propose to give you magic formulas or a genie in a lamp, but I do intend to debunk some myths and provide a framework for you to achieve competence in employing hedge fund techniques. The definition of a hedge fund has certainly begun to migrate, but at the end of the day you, like most investors, would like to earn profits irrespective of market conditions or direction. That's what a hedge fund is supposed to do. There are a host of investment vehicles you can employ to do the same thing that hedge funds do. I intend to show you some of your options. More important, I would like to provide a structure whereby you can continue learning and employing these techniques for your own benefit. The providers are not better at it than you are. They simply have had greater exposure.

Mind you, hedge funds lose money, too. Losing money is an indelible reality of making money. You want more of the latter and less of the former. As many a colleague has related to me, "I had to leave the firm. I couldn't make money on the trading desk because they wouldn't let me lose any money. As soon as a trade went south, they would cut me, practically ensuring a loss time after time." Pure arbitrage (a trade without risk in which you simultaneously buy and sell something for a profit) does not really exist anymore, but if you are prudent, I think I can help you meet your investment goals.

After my finance internship, I actually did go to medical school for some time, but the call of the financial markets in the 1980s was too strong to resist. I was guaranteed a job by one of the investment banks even after I matriculated to medical school. It was a great deal because I was compensated whether I showed up or not. Eventually the hours and toil of working the job and going to medical school was too much, so I resigned from medical school and dove headlong into finance. The rest is history.

Today I run a hedge fund. Over the years I have slugged it out in the financial markets and learned a lot of lessons. I have made mistakes and also hit some huge home runs. I want to share some of the strategies that I've developed with you.

There are so many instruments and strategies and investments and styles available to the average person today that, armed with a few disciplines, you will soon be competing with the bigger funds and maybe even outperforming them. That is my goal in this book—to strip away the veils of mystery and obfuscation that have surrounded hedge funds and help you, the average investor, generate the skills and confidence to compete with the big boys.

Do-It-Yourself
HEDGE
FUNDS

CHAPTER 1

INVESTABLE INSTRUMENTS

Sometimes I sit in my office in midtown Manhattan and marvel at all the tall buildings around me. Each one teems with financial professionals who are focused on one thing: investing in the financial markets. Finance is to New York what movies are to Hollywood. Thousands and thousands of the best and the brightest minds are collected on the tiny (and tony) island of Manhattan, focused intently and obsessively on investments. The tall buildings in London, Los Angeles, Paris, Munich, Japan, Frankfurt, and every other major (and developing) city across the globe also teem with smart people focused intently on the same thing: investing and profiting in the financial markets.

One has to wonder, with all of the millions of participants and the trillions of dollars that they have at their disposal, how in the world is it possible to discern and implement an idea in the financial markets that no one has thought of before? Forget about being unique. How can one identify investment ideas that will remain profitable when so many others, both locally and abroad, are poring over the same opportunities?

Some market theorists would argue that the markets are efficient. In an efficient market, an investor cannot really outperform the normal stock indexes, like the Dow 30 or the

S&P 500 Index. No matter how enlightened your stock selections, the efficient-market theorists believe that the market will eventually outperform you. There is some truth to this. Take a look at the average investment manager, and nine times out of ten the S&P 500 outperforms him.

The efficient-market theorists would argue that all market information is known, available, understood, and measured by the market. Given that most market participants are aware of the same risks and opportunities, there are no free lunches or secret opportunities. When all the good opportunities are known, everybody piles on and achieves the same return. Perfect knowledge, then, enables an investor to market perform, while less-than-perfect knowledge dooms an investor to underperform the market.

Suppose you did find an investment idea that was unique and profitable. That insight wouldn't last for long. Like the pileup of tacklers in a football game, other market participants would eventually learn and perfect your idea and drive the profitability out of it. Sometimes the latecomers even overdemand the opportunity, which can create a bubble. In the end you are either long on the trade opportunity (which means you own it) or you are not. The expected outcome is not absolutely certain, but the market establishes a consensus for both the reward (the price return) and the risk (the potential loss or variability in that expectation). The potential for risk and reward are already reflected in the price you would pay. The efficient-market theorists argue that over the long term, the market consensus is always right, and cannot be beaten.

I am on the side that argues that the market is inefficient. This position is not necessarily inconsistent with those who believe in efficient markets; it depends upon the time frame of reference. If an investor were to purchase a static portfolio of stocks, then the efficient-market theory would hold true. Any buy-and-hold strategy would have difficulty out-performing the broad market indices, like the S&P 500 or the Russell 1000. But there are many other ways to play the market besides buy and hold. Indeed, today there are investors who trade 100 percent turnover a day with just seconds separating each trade. There are quasimarket makers who reap a "riskless" profit with every trade they make. So while it is true that market information is widely available, investors' rate of information uptake is asymmetrical; it is based on the timing of its dissemination, a person's ability to understand the information, risk preference, capital availability (cost), mood, greed, skill, and so on. Irrespective of the known market data, there are pricing dislocations—both short term and long term—that occur in real time that can offer great profit opportunities.

The prospect of market efficiency assumes that market participants learn of and use information intelligently, immediately, and at the same time. It does not happen that way. For example, every investor knew that the technology market was overvalued in 1999. The NASDAQ was surging in 1999, from 1050 in December 1995 to a high of 5048 in March of 2000, an average annual return of 48 percent per year. *Everyone* knew it was a bubble; companies without profits—and without revenue, for that matter—were trading in the tens if not hundreds of millions of dollars in value. StarMedia, for example, was an exciting start-up, promising a Spanish-language Web site for Latin Americans. It was a great idea. Before it could even squeak out a decent spate of revenue, StarMedia debuted at a valuation of $1.2 billion. In 1999, at its peak, it was valued at $3.9 billion. In 2002, after the bubble, StarMedia was sold to the Spanish Internet provider eresMas Interactive for $8 million cash. Intelligence in this atmosphere did not prevail; the lust for profit—greed, in other words—hindered rational thinking. My point is that dislocations and mispricings can and frequently do occur for discrete periods. Certainly, the markets are inefficient periodically.

Somewhere in those shiny buildings in cities all around the world are another subset of investors, the Quants. Quants, or quantitative analysts, use primarily quantitative techniques rather than intuition or discretion to evaluate and effect market bets. They do not read annual reports or use discretion in constructing their strategies. In many cases, because computers select their portfolios, the managers may not even know the contents of their portfolios. The Quants are devotees of Arbitrage Pricing Theory, Capital Asset Pricing Models, Black-Scholes models, Markowitz optimizations, cointegration models, factor models, Bayesian Algorithms, neural nets, and the like.

Quant approaches generally benefit from the inherent market inefficiencies that may not be visible to the naked eye. I have been a fan of the quant strategies because they eliminate the emotional component of investing and depend exclusively on the rational, concrete calculations of hard data. I always felt that I could count on the computer to have consistent judgment; human beings, on the other hand, have weaknesses: fatigue, emotionally driven escalations of commitment, the need to party, domestic problems, etc.

Quants deploy mathematical models to not only identify market inefficiencies but to trade on them in a structured way, eliminating the human element from their trading. These structured algorithms—predesigned, rule-based, often computer driven decision-making schemes—seek out price dislocations, whether they are short term (milliseconds) or long term (months), with a cool, calculated precision.

The financial markets also have their share of Chartists,

who look at the markets like Rorschach tests—"blots" of historical market performance. Embedded in the historical price actions of securities are various "formations"—head and shoulders,[1] double tops,[2] resistance points,[3] etc.—and as a result Chartists believe they can project how the market is going to move in the near future. A projection like that would be a valuable tool because it would enable the investor to position his trade to profit from the next tick. But in my opinion, Chartists are not always so accurate since their insights are based upon hindsight. They are about as accurate as the average weatherman. Don't bother to bring your umbrella.

Inside traders deserve a mention. These are the rogues of the lot, trading upon ill-gotten information that only trusted fiduciaries know. They come upon inside information through illicit means or simply through a breach of trust of sensitive information in order to make a trade with a guaranteed profit. This can obviously be an enormously profitable investment strategy. The only drawback is that it is illegal. If you knew ahead of time that Bear Stearns would collapse or that the Fed would raise interest rates or that the Pentagon was ready to award a lucrative contract, imagine the profits you could make by being able to trade on that information without risk! Some of the most successful practitioners of trading using inside information have had commensurate sentences in federal prison, because they are crooks.

---

1. Head and shoulders pattern is a technical analysis term used to describe a chart formation in which a stock's price: a) Rises to a peak and subsequently declines; b) then rises above the former peak and again declines; then c) rises again, but not to the second peak, and declines once more. [Investopedia].
2. Double top is a term used in technical analysis to describe the rise of a stock, a drop, another rise to the same level as the original rise, and finally another drop. [Investopedia]
3. Resistance is the price at which a stock or market can trade but not exceed for a certain period of time. Often referred to as "resistance level." [Investopedia]

Recently Bernard Ebbers (WorldCom) and Jeff Skilling (Enron) each received long prison sentences for securities fraud and trading on insider information, respectively. Ebbers was sentenced to twenty-five years in prison for his role in the record $11 billion accounting fraud that brought down World-Com,[4] while Skilling was sentenced to more than twenty-four years in prison for his role in the collapse of Enron, which had a peak market cap of $66 billion. Even Martha Stewart spent a little time in the Big House for an amount that is comparably infinitesimal. Martha Stewart's real offense was lying to federal agents, but the transaction in question was a mere $45,000. Most recently, a jury found the former Credit Suisse banker Hafiz Muhammad Zubair Naseem guilty of one count of conspiracy and twenty-eight counts of insider trading for relaying insider information to Ajaz Rahim, a high-level banker in Pakistan.[5] Not everyone gets caught, though. I knew of a trader at a well-known investment house who routinely received timely "tips" from his friends on merger activity. He converted very small positions to million-dollar payouts more than once.

Insider trading is not only perpetrated by insiders. In the 1980s, there was the enterprising Merrill Lynch broker William Dillon, who traded stocks based on articles in advance copies of *BusinessWeek* magazine. That was 1988. Ten years later another broker executed almost the exact same scam again! Eugene Plotkin, a former Goldman Sachs associate, formed a network that traded on sensitive information gleaned from, you guessed it, an analyst at Merrill Lynch and pre-publication issues of *BusinessWeek* magazine. Plotkin pleaded

---

4. *New York Times*, "Ebbers Sentenced to 25 Years in Prison for $11 Billion Fraud," July 13, 2005.
5. *New York Times*, "Former Banker Convicted of Insider Trading," February 5, 2008.

guilty to one count each of conspiracy to commit securities fraud, insider trading, and felony criminal contempt in connection with violating a grand jury oath of secrecy.

And so on, and so on. There are scores of other characters in the financial markets with their own idiosyncrasies too numerous to mention. The short of it is that the financial markets are crowded. A vast group of market players sits at the table, looking for the same opportunities to turn a profit. Their activities will collectively have a direct impact on your own ability to make money.

The Homegrown Trader

Until relatively recently an individual needed to be wealthy to have the privilege of a stockbroker. Today, the average investor can open a brokerage account online in seconds. As a result, there are a lot more eyeballs scouring the markets. Thus, over the last twenty years, there has been a significant increase in the daily volume of stock trading. Take a look below at the charted history of the S&P 500 Index. Starting in 1995, the S&P 500 began a steep upward trend. This "up" regime of market performance was concurrent with the beginning of the market's interest in technology companies (America Online, for example) as well as the growth of individuals' trading access. Concurrent with the index's advancement, there is a substantial increase in the volume of shares traded, represented by the shaded blue area at the bottom right of the graph. It illustrates a parabolic explosion of increased volume and market activity.

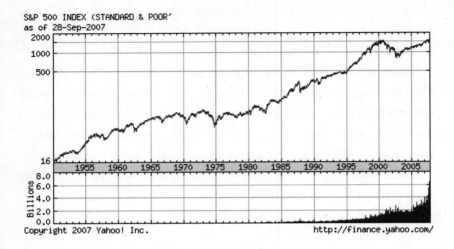

S&P 500 INDEX (STANDARD & POOR'
as of 28-Sep-2007

Copyright 2007 Yahoo! Inc.   http://finance.yahoo.com/

This graph illustrates a few other interesting points. First, the efficient-market crowd would point out that an investor would do quite well to have simply bought the S&P 500 Index and forgotten about trying to trade to beat the market. On the whole, the S&P 500 has yielded a pretty attractive return over time. Sure, there were a few bumps along the way, but for patient, long-term investors, the market return has been competitive. A passive S&P 500 investor would have tripled his investment between 1995 and 2007, by buying an S&P 500 mutual fund. Proponents of the market's inefficiency propose, however, that the bumps, the variability of the index day to day, month to month, ignored by the "efficient" passive crowd, present huge profit opportunities. Market dislocations do happen, and they can be profitable if you know they're there and how to benefit from them.

The market conspires to prove that by buying anything other than an S&P 500 mutual fund, you will yield an inferior return. And for the most part, that is true. Only approximately 10 percent of all long-only managers outperform the S&P 500 Index. The other 90 percent are all dedicated, educated, and smart people, but the odds are that the market will outperform them. They will, nonetheless, collect their fees. I used to be quite amused by the *Wall Street Journal* dartboard, where more often than not a portfolio comprised by throwing a dart randomly at a list of stocks would outperform portfolios selected by professional money managers. The success of the dartboard may be the reason why the newspaper discontinued the feature. There are some managers who almost never make money but manage vast sums of money and earn, if that's the right word, sizable management fees. I cannot figure out how they stay in business . . . but they do. I think you, the reader, can do as well on your own, even if only by taking the passive route.

But it is a challenge. For every security you would sell or buy, there is someone on the other side of the trade who believes just the opposite of what you do. All of the other investors just like you add up to a vast collection of opinions otherwise known as the Market. It is difficult to "hear" one opinion in the racket of the Market, but taken together, the Market yields an indelible harmony that is difficult to outdo. Indeed, to outperform the market consistently takes an enormous amount of skill.

With the admitted difficulty of outperforming the market at all, I will attempt to show you how to create your own hedge fund strategies. This is an undertaking, but by adhering to simple principles, I can put you in a position to at least compete.

We should start by considering the fundamentals of what makes a hedge strategy. One of the fundamental, distinguishing characteristics of a hedge strategy is a virtually unlimited investment universe. What I mean is that the hedge manager is compelled to consider a vast range of investment securities. Vast and complex as these financial instruments are, they generally fall into three main categories: stocks, bonds, and commodities/futures.

Nature and Her Assets

Whether you believe in Darwinism or Intelligent Design, the original assets that make all market activity possible are the earth and sun. Don't laugh. It is the yield from these two assets that drives the world economy. Nature provides the raw fuels for a company's growth, such as consumable goods (grains, water), labor (human capital, beasts of burden), and energy (potential and kinetic energy, oil, heat). From an historical perspective, the cultivation of natural assets made it possible for us humans to evolve from hunter-gatherers to civilized people. Instead of hunting barefoot and hungry for each meal, we were able to harvest the "free" production of the earth by farming. A civilization that can cultivate, store, and distribute food no longer requires that all of its subjects should hunt. Hunting and gathering wild food were activities that would consume the majority of effort and time for the hunter-gatherer. When the whole population was no longer required to hunt, the *sedentary population*—those that were no longer required to hunt—pursued other activities, such as textile making, home building, art, and military technology.[6]

Another name for nature's assets is *commodities*, and they are tradable in the hedge fund manager's playbook. Commodities include basic resources and agricultural products, such as iron, crude oil, coal, ethanol, sugar, soybeans, hogs, beef, aluminum, rice, wheat, gold, and silver. The labor leverage implicit in the earth's production of commodities and our ability to enhance and control its yield is what has led to the development of civilization as we know it.

---

6. See Jared Diamond, *Guns, Germs and Steel*.

Do not overlook the impact and importance of commodities when considering any potential investment strategy. The total volume in commodities traded daily is tens of billions of dollars. Every company in which you might consider investing is somehow directly dependent upon the consumption of commodities. Therefore the prices, and the trends in prices, for commodities will directly affect the profitability of any company you might consider. Commodities have a bearing upon every one of your trading ideas. Trading commodities will be a tool for your hedge strategy, either directly by trading actual commodities, or indirectly by trading companies that are active in commodities.

Real Assets Versus Financial Assets

There are two principal types of investment assets available to the investor—real assets and financial assets. In simple terms, real assets are those that one can touch or hold, such as real estate, automobiles, airplanes, metals, fine stones, and jewelry. Financial assets are those that derive their value from labor, such as services, labor, intellectual property, and common stocks. Throughout history the growth of organized societies fueled the need for financial assets. With financial assets, such as currency, came the ability to trade using a recognized conduit to convey value.

Financial assets derive their value from their underlying productive capacity. The ownership of a restaurant company has the capacity to generate revenue, for example, and would therefore represent a financial asset. The restaurant would make use of real assets to generate revenue for its owner, including the real estate on which the restaurant conducts its business, the kitchen machinery used to prepare the foods, and the cars used to deliver the food to the surrounding neighborhood. The restaurant also makes use of almost all

the aforementioned commodities, including the grain to create the final products; the energy to prepare its food and to
innervate the premises; the metals for pans, stoves, sinks, and
knives. Still, *ownership* of the company is a financial asset.
Therefore, financial assets derive their value from the exploi-
tation of real assets. The ownership of a financial asset, such
as company stock, represents the "right" to participate in the
production of revenue and therefore profit from the utilization of real assets. The real assets in this restaurant enterprise
would be referred to as book value. The term "book value" is
used to describe the practice of accounting for purchases of
real assets in the "book" of the business enterprise.

A quick story on the importance of book value. One of my
friends from Stanford School of Business, Bill Browder, is
one of the most successful hedge fund managers in the world
and an early pioneer in investing in eastern Europe. He is the
founder of Hermitage Capital Management, which generated
2,500 percent returns to its investors over a ten-year period.
But his beginning was inauspicious.

Intelligent, bright-eyed, and ambitious, Bill joined the London office of Salomon Brothers investment bank in the early
1990s, not long after graduating from business school. Salomon Brothers had a reputation for having a hard-charging environment. It had clawed itself up the ranks of the investment
banks through the sheer grittiness of its bond-trading operations. In fact, Salomon Brothers was a snarling snake pit of
naked Wall Street ambition. The bank was not really known
for corporate investment banking, however, so when Bill arrived, there was no mentor, no welcome, no training program,
no secretary, no love. The new bosses even seemed a bit surprised when he showed up on his first day. They showed him
to his desk, pointed him to the telephone, and shoved a box

of business cards into his chest. "And by the way," they noted earnestly, "you will need to generate fees at least four times what we are paying you or you will be fired." Rising to the challenge, Bill set about looking for ways to earn four times his salary.

But the going was tough. One of the rules when working in a snake pit is that territory is staked out pretty aggressively. Each cohort banker claims his territory, his business opportunities, like a dog would mark a fire hydrant. Each time Bill seemed to get a great idea about how to develop business, some senior banker would let him know in no uncertain terms that he was unwelcome. As a consequence, all of the choice ideas and clients in western Europe were already taken.

"It'll be tough but maybe I can do something in eastern Europe," he thought nervously after several months of generating goose eggs in fees. He had heard rumors that Salomon Brothers was holding an internal meeting to discuss the privatization of Malév Hungarian Airlines. "That sounds pretty promising." The fact that he had had to rely on the rumor should have been a clear signal that he was not invited. "We are all on the same team," he shrugged, and managed to find out where the meeting was being held so that he could scout for potential business.

When Bill walked into the room it was as if a steaming sack of garlic was sitting on top of his head. He walked over to a chair as the room of bankers silently glared at his every step. It was like the EF Hutton commercial of old: the music and conversations stopped, and people looked up, visibly annoyed, as if to say, "What the hell are you doing here?" Of course he was not welcome. The Salomon bankers in the room were trying to earn four times their *own* pay. That goal would certainly be in jeopardy if another banker were allowed in. They pulled him aside. "Whoever you are, we have enough people here to get this done. Thanks." Bill quietly slithered out of the room, and the conversations ensued, undeterred, without him.

A couple days later he heard again of an internal discussion regarding the privatization of the main Polish telecommunications company. This time Bill thought he would be more aggressive. He would insert himself into this meeting in a manner consistent with the aggressive character of his cohorts. But the bankers on the Polish transaction were equally aggressive about telling him to get lost. This time, they yelled from their seats. "Not only are you not welcome here, but don't even think of *flying* over Poland."

Exasperated and perhaps resigned to failure, Bill decided that he had to stake out an area of opportunity that was not yet claimed by his ophidian colleagues. Russia was an area where Salomon had zero banking activity, and for good reason: there was none to be done. Nonetheless, Bill loudly declared himself the banker for Russia at the Monday-morning meeting and waited for his phone to ring so yet another senior banker could curse at him to stay away. The phone never rang, and Bill officially became the Russia banker for Salomon Brothers. No matter that there was no business—he finally had a territory of his own! But the only intelligence on Russia that the bank had was a (short) list of "dead" or failed, transactions. It was like selling panties to Britney Spears.

Starting from scratch, he spent weeks fruitlessly pursuing meetings, networking, going to conferences, and cold calling, but nothing worked. Eventually Bill got a nibble. The management of a Russian fishing fleet wanted advice on whether to purchase their company as part of Russia's privatization program. They had asked a UK law firm to contact all of the major investment banks and to encourage those banks to submit a proposal.

Bill knew nothing about fishing (or Russia, for that matter).

And Salomon Brothers had no experience in fishing industries other than a smattering of advisory assignments that they had conducted for the Japanese whaling industry fifteen to twenty years prior. Desperate, Bill used his best fiction-writing skills and concocted a proposal that suggested he could advise the fleet competently as compared with his competitors.

Bill is convinced that his was the only presentation submitted because the very next day, he received a phone call. "Mr. Browder? We would like to hire you to advise us on this transaction. But first we have to negotiate fees." "Oh, jeez," Bill thought. They continued, "We will pay you $50,000 for two months' consultation." It was, indeed, a short negotiation. Now, to give some perspective, supermodel Linda Evangelista famously declared that she would not even get out of bed for less than $10,000 per day. Certainly no investment banker would get out of a Bentley for a paltry $50,000 fee over *two months*. But $50,000 was better than the zero he had earned thus far, so Bill took the assignment.

The headquarters of the fishing fleet was a town called Murmansk, located in the extreme northwestern part of Russia, with a seaport on Kola Bay, not far from Russia's borders with Norway and Finland. As far as distance goes, it is about as north as one can physically go on the globe. Even Santa Claus doesn't go that far north. The only way to get there was a four-and-a-half-hour flight to St. Petersburg, which arrived at 9:00 p.m., then a trip in a small Soviet-era plane that took off at 4:00 a.m. for Murmansk. On the approach to Murmansk, the flight was diverted because there were large potholes in the runway at the Murmansk airport. One can only imagine how big the holes must have been that they were too large to risk landing the airplane there. So the plane was forced to land at a nearby—classified—military airbase amongst rows of rusted-out MiGs.

The director of the fishing fleet met him at the airport. Browder did not know anything about the company other than that it was a fishing fleet. Preparation for the meeting was not possible, inasmuch as telephones could not reach the town of Murmansk, and there was absolutely no publicly available information about the company. Over dinner the director finally shared with Bill the capital dilemma they faced. Through the privatization program, the employees had the right to buy 51 percent of the book value of the company for $2.5 million. They were not sure whether or not they should exercise it.

"That's it?" Bill was exasperated, defeated. He had come a long, hard journey only to learn that he had run into yet another dead end. Sure the fee was only $50,000 but he had hoped it at least would have been a noteworthy transaction. With his head in his hands, fearing for his future, he glanced at the shipyard. "Who owns all of those?" he asked, gesturing toward the ships at port. "Well, we do, Gaspadin Browder." Book value had just become a lot more interesting.

It turns out that the fishing company owned one hundred ships, each of which had been purchased new for $20 million. The fishing company therefore was in possession of a total value of $2 billion in ships at replacement cost. The fleet was less than half depreciated, leaving more than $1 billion in total marketable value if the company decided to sell the fleet. And management had the right to buy the ships for $2.5 million, the book value of the ships!

The reason for this disparity was that the book value of the fleet was negotiated in rubles several years prior, at a time when the dollar/ruble exchange rate was much higher. Because of hyperinflation, the ruble had since been devalued one thousand times, so that the ruble was worth 1/1000 its value as of the signing of the privatization agreement.

The answer was an emphatic "Yes!" Bill advised them to acquire the company as soon as humanly possible. He still collected only his $50,000 fee (and a bottle of Sputnik Vodka), but a light went off that this transaction could be repeated all over the country. Why collect lowly advisory fees of $50,000 when he could spend more time trying to buy $1 billion companies for $5 million? Thus, Hermitage was born. Today, Hermitage has approximately $3 billion in investments and a lifetime average annual return of more than 30 percent.

When book value becomes disconnected from market value, there is a compelling opportunity for the trader. In the case of Russia, you had an entire nation with such a disconnect. As part of its privatization, the government issued 150 million vouchers to the People, representing 30 percent of the total value of Russia's private industries. Each voucher had a market price of about $20. Do the math, and that comes to $3 billion, implying a total industry valuation of $10 billion. By comparison, the market capitalization of those industries today is more than $1.5 *trillion*, or 150 times the original book value.

As an interesting note, Bill's family did not exactly have a history in capitalism. His grandfather, Earl Browder, was famous in the United States in the 1930s and 1940s as the general secretary of the American Communist Party and was twice an aspirant to the presidency. Sometimes the apple does, indeed, fall far from the tree. As testimony to Bill's success as a capitalist, "the government of President Vladimir Putin has barred him from entering Russia under Federal Law No. 114FZ. The statute lets Russia exclude people who might threaten 'the security of the state, public order or public health.'"

The takeaway is that financial assets, while intangible, derive value from a company's utilization of real assets and labor. Real assets are the building blocks for the generation of financial asset value. It is when the two become diametrically untethered—or when they crescendo harmoniously—that investment opportunities arise. This is one of the "dislocations" that hedge managers seek to identify.

Occasionally, book value can be grossly overstated. In March 2008, Bear Stearns' share price collapsed in a stunning and precipitous decline in value—to $30 a share. Even then, Bear Stearns had a book value of more than $11 billion. I know of many hedge funds that stepped in and bought Bear Stearns at $30 per share—already sharply down from its high of $170 per share—because, they theorized, the book value was a minimum of $80 a share. Thirty dollars per share was therefore a bargain. This Browderian purchase of shares at "below" book value did not pay off: a few trading days later, the shares were worth only $2 each. Ouch! The book value did not go away; it is simply that the "Browder" play (that's a new term in finance) was had by JPMorgan, who was able to snap up the entire company in an acquisition for $10 per share to the chagrin of the early speculators.

The Key Financial Assets for Your Hedge Universe

The return on every financial asset can be broken down into two components: capital appreciation and cash flow. Capital appreciation is the increase (or decrease) in the price of an asset over the purchase price. Cash flow is the actual cash distributions to the owner.

To go back to the restaurant, for example, your ownership value could increase in two ways: first, the difference in price that a buyer would be willing to pay you for your ownership of the restaurant versus your own purchase cost; second, the amount of cash or dividend paid to the owner out of profits. The sum of the two is your total return on the financial asset.

Specifically, if you purchase a restaurant for $100,000 and would be able to sell it a year later for $200,000, that would constitute capital appreciation. This type of appreciation is realized by disposing of the asset. Prior to sale, the capital appreciation is implied but not realized and is known as the unrealized gain. So if, a year after you bought it, you know that the restaurant is worth $200,000 but decide to keep the restaurant, you would have an unrealized gain of $100,000, or 100 percent. During the course of the same year, the restaurant may have thrown off some cash to you. That cash flow represents a source of return known as a dividend. The restaurant therefore provides two sources of return: capital appreciation, which continues to grow (or decline) for as long as you hold the asset but remains unrealized until it is disposed of, and the cash flow, which comes to you as a result of holding the asset.

Each year, the capital appreciation will fluctuate, depending on revenue production, profitability, demand, and the competitiveness of the restaurant. The cash flow that you take home after expenses is your dividend (or coupon). Your dividend will depend on the profitability of the business as well as your decision about how much of the excess cash to pay out to yourself. The cash paid out to you, the owner, is known as the dividend payout. The benefit of cash to the owner is that it may be used immediately for other productive purposes, such as purchases or other investments, while capital appreciation is not unlocked until the owner sells (or borrows against) his ownership. The business may also decide to retain cash—i.e., no dividend payouts—which can be valuable to reinvest into the business for even greater and more accelerated capital appreciation, such as expansion, renovation, or the opening of a new restaurant. In the real world, companies are always measuring the perceived value of paying out profits to owners versus reinvesting available cash to help grow the business.

With these definitions in mind, we are now ready to investigate the simplest building blocks for your hedge portfolio.

Stocks, Bonds, and Commodities

In your universe of potential investment opportunities, there are three basic financial instruments available: common stock (or equity), bonds (or debt), and commodities. There are thousands of other instruments and variants, but they all derive their value from one of these three fundamental investment categories.

Stocks and bonds are financial assets that derive their value from the productive capacity of a company. Companies use real assets (machinery, factories, raw goods, commodities) plus labor to generate products and services for sale, which generates revenue and income for the company's shareholders. Revenue minus the cost of conducting business equals profit. The percentage of profit paid to its owners represents the dividend payout.

Companies raise money, or "capital," to increase their capacity to generate products and services and therefore generate more profit. The proceeds from raising capital are used to buy new equipment and to hire more people, the building blocks of company growth. Companies can raise money by offering either bonds and stock to investors who wish to participate in the future potential value growth of the company and benefit from its capital appreciation. When an investor purchases a stock or a bond (in the primary market), the transaction provides money to the company for its intended growth in return for a stake in the company's future.

The way in which the company compensates the investor for participation differs substantially between the stock and bond. Each instrument represents a stake in the future of the company through a distinctly different "basket of rights."

Common Stocks

The entitlement of common stock holders is the net cash flow and net assets of the company after all expenses and liabilities have been paid. If there is nothing left after all expenses are paid, then the common stock holders get nothing. If the company grows as anticipated, its value will greatly exceed the sum of its liabilities and offer a handsome capital appreciation as well as annual cash flow to the common stock holder.

By buying a share of common stock, you, the investor, become a part owner in the company that has issued the stock. Your ownership percentage can be calculated by dividing the number of shares you own by the total shares outstanding. Chances are it is only a tiny fraction—but it still represents ownership. As a result, the stockholder's return is at risk, just like any other business owner's. The value of a shareholder's investment depends on the increase in real assets that the company owns, plus its current and future profits. By these measures, the value of a share of common stock will increase or decrease.

Think of a company whose stock you buy as a business partner in the way you would think of any partner. If your enterprise makes money, you should get a distribution of cash, a dividend. If the enterprise is failing relative to your competitors, you should justifiably express concern. If the company does not improve you can express your discontent to management or even fire management with the help of other like-minded shareholders.[7] Alternatively, you can vote with your feet by selling your ownership to someone else. You would not tolerate a lazy, absent, or incompetent business partner in real life. Nor should you do so with the management of

---

7. Active shareholders are increasingly common, part of a hedge fund movement known as "activist investing."

the companies whose shares you own. Hold management accountable, no matter how small your investment.

Common stock valuation is a topic of vast proportions, so we will not discuss the textbook details here. There are volumes of theories to consider on stock valuation: Graham and Dodd, modern portfolio theory, arbitrage pricing theory, dividend discount models, and so on. Common sense applies, too, and it is one of the most powerful valuation models of all. Too many investors fall prey to the "last fool" trap: they buy a stock at a certain price with little consideration of the reasonableness of its current value. They hope to sell later to another market sucker. Ideally, you own a particular stock because, at that price, you would be happy to have management as your business partner.

Bonds

Bonds also derive value from the revenue-producing capacity of a company. Like stocks, bonds are issued by companies to raise operating capital. As we have noted, the companies pay a fixed interest rate, i.e., equal, sequential cash payments to the bondholders. Bondholders are the first to be reimbursed even if a company fails to be profitable. The decision to buy stocks versus bonds largely depends on your appetite for risks and rewards. Investors in need of the surety of fixed income generally prefer a high concentration of bonds in their investment portfolios.

Bondholders are the first to be paid, but their participation is limited to a fixed cash flow calculated as a percentage of their money invested, usually referred to as a coupon. Bondholders therefore do not participate in the great potential for capital appreciation of the company. This is why bond payouts are known as fixed income. The advantage to holding bonds, however, is that if the company fails to turn a profit the bondholders still get paid. And if a company fails completely and is forced to liquidate, the bondholders are still first in line to get their capital out. This is not a trivial matter when a company founders.

Holding bonds can also be an exercise in remorse, nonetheless when companies are very successful. While the common stock holders enjoy hefty multiples of return on their investments, as they have, say, in Apple or Microsoft, the bondholders do not participate because they are limited to fixed payments, the coupon. Common stock holders in the aforementioned companies earned as much as one hundred times their original investment, while bondholders ambled along with a paltry annual coupon of 7 percent or so.

The price of the bond may vary based on general market conditions for debt and interest rates (and certainly the overall health of the underlying company). But generally the variations are small, so the primary source of return is the cash payout or interest rate.

Commodities

Commodities prices are a direct result of demand. Two of the most commonly traded commodities are gold and energy. As of this writing, the price of gold has surged to more than $1,000 per ounce, a record level for the shiny metal. It is favored to increase further—a beneficiary of the present inflationary environment in the U.S. An investor looking to trade in gold has nothing to consider other than current economic conditions, demand, and the current trend in gold's price. There are no companies directly associated with the price of gold, and gold does not have a CEO or a board of directors. The reason to buy the gold commodity today is that it hedges inflation and has a strongly positive secular trend as a result. The demand for gold is high, so its price will go higher. There is something refreshingly pure about the pricing of commodities as a direct result of their supply and demand.

Similarly, the current demand for oil is the highest it's ever been, recently topping $145 per barrel. Many reputable analysts are predicting that it will approach $200 a barrel in the near future. The U.S. demand for oil, the largest of any sovereign nation, is at its highest levels ever, while at the same time developing economies such as India and China are consuming more exponentially. In a matter of years, transportation in in some areas of China went from 80 percent bicycles to 80 percent cars. Such demand has led to the highest price levels for oil in history. In 2006, just two years ago, the average price for a barrel of oil was $21.66, a six-fold increase. As with all commodities, including gold, its value derives strictly from the balances and imbalances of supply and demand. The rise (and rise) of oil, in which the astute investor could have participated, has been driven by global economic demand, perception, and projection, not company analysis.

Mutual Funds

It is a stretch to call a mutual fund a derivative product, although that is technically what it is. Mutual funds became popular as a way for smaller investors to benefit from scale. Often I am asked, for example, "I have five thousand dollars saved. How should I invest it?"

That's the problem. Size matters. The average investor does not have a large nest egg, which is one of the cultural mores that distinguishes Americans.[8] Still, for the savings we do have, we want stock, or bond market exposure. So there exists a real scale issue.

Suppose you want to buy a diversified portfolio of stocks. A

---

8. The United States has one of the lowest savings rates in the developed world. Besides compromising the nation's ability to withstand slower economic times, a low savings rate reduces the ability to invest in infrastructure. That is one of the reasons Americans must borrow from other countries in order to support their lifestyles.

diversified portfolio is preferable to a portfolio of only a few positions because it diversifies away the impact of a loss in any one position. The more stocks you have in your portfolio, the less susceptible the portfolio is to the change in value of any one particular company. A diversified portfolio, over time, will usually outperform a concentrated portfolio. The problem is that obtaining a portfolio of diversified stocks requires a lot of money, exceeding the capital available to the average investor.

For example, the average price of a NYSE large capitalization stock is about $40. If you wanted to buy a portfolio of fifty stocks and one hundred shares of each stock, it would require $200,000 *minimum*. That is well beyond the cash availability of most investors.

Thus, mutual funds give the average investor the chance to invest smaller sums of money while still achieving a diversified portfolio. Since mutual funds technically allow for the ownership of fractional shares and no minimum lots, even a $5,000 investment could "participate" in a portfolio costing many times more in total. The mutual fund is a convenient way to give the smaller investor access to multiple stock positions and, for that matter, the benefit of a professional money manager. It has been demonstrated that a portfolio of mutual funds can outperform or perform equally as well as most actively managed portfolios.

Mutual funds can be of great value to the individual investor, but they also have a few annoying limitations. First, they are valued only once per day after the close of the stock market. As intra-day market volatility and volume increase, the difference between a mutual fund's start-of-day and end-of-day value becomes wider and wider. If the market were collapsing, a mutual fund investor could only look wistfully as the market declined without being able to change his investment exposure. By the time the day had come to an end, Armageddon could have occurred while the mutual fund investor could only have watched.

Mutual funds are also limited in terms of leverage, as it is not possible to short sell a mutual fund, a practice whereby the holder sells a borrowed security with the hopes of buying it back at a lower price. But increasingly, mutual funds do offer lots of choices for the individual investor—specific sector exposure, country-level baskets of stocks, and emerging market portfolios.

Exchange-Traded Funds

Exchange-traded funds (ETFs) are mutual funds on steroids. Just like mutual funds, ETFs aggregate the smaller investor's capital so he can acquire a larger portfolio with little money. ETFs eliminate the problem of the end-of-day pricing endemic to mutual funds because ETFs are updated in real-time, tick by tick, in lockstep with the change in market price of their underlying securities. ETFs make intraday basket trading possible for the small investor. An investor wishing to have tactical asset exposure for short periods of time can do so. Moreover, ETFs can be shorted. An investor who wants negative exposure to a particular asset class can get it with an ETF. There are a few standouts in ETFs. The quadruple-Qs (QQQQ), the Spiders (SPDR), and the Diamonds Trust Series 1 (DIA)—ETFs for the Nasdaq 100 Index, the S&P 500 Index, and the Dow Jones Industrial Average index respectively—are among the most traded ETFs by volume.

The ETF is worth the average price of all its constituents and can be bought and sold at any time during the day. So if an investor wanted long exposure in the market in the morning and short exposure in the afternoon, he could get it. The development of ETFs was a very powerful innovation for the average investor, allowing him to get varied exposure to different slices of the market priced on a real-time basis. Moreover, if an investor would rather hold shares than the ETF, the ETF is redeemable for the underlying shares upon request. Many hedge fund managers with various trading styles increasingly use ETFs to get tactical exposure to a sector, an industry, or a theme.

Futures

Futures contracts for commodities have existed for centuries. Trading in commodities began in Japan in the eighteenth century to facilitate the trading of rice and silk. They are essentially an agreement made today, between a buyer and seller, to exchange "real goods," commodities, at some future date at a specified price. For example, a farmer may want to know today exactly how much money he will make on his future crop yield. He may want to lock in that price, and collect it today, perhaps because he needs to offset the impending costs of production. So he would seek a willing buyer today, even before the crop is reaped, at a discount to his expected future price, taking into account market risk and prevailing interest rates, and collect the money today.

In addition to agricultural futures, there are also financial futures which were introduced in the 1970s by the Chicago Mercantile Exchange (CME). The launch of these "derivatives" was very successful and quickly overtook commodities futures in trading volume. Financial futures are similar to commodities futures, except that the deliverables are cash instead of real goods like corn or hogs. A future on the S&P 500, for example, is a contract between a buyer and seller to exchange the difference between the value of the S&P 500 today versus the value of the S&P 500 at some future date. For example if I buy the S&P 500 future and the S&P 500 increases, then the seller owes me the difference upon expiration. If the S&P 500 decreases, then I must pay the difference. The face value of one contract of an S&P 500 future is $250 multiplied by the value of the index, presently around $350,000.

The total universe of financial futures available span multiple markets, and each future contract has unique specifications. Futures are a way to gain tactical exposure to a certain market, say the United Kingdom, without having to buy every one of the stocks in that market. If you believe that the entire stock market is going to increase/decrease, a financial future would be a way to express that view. The sheer size of the contract makes it less likely a tool for the small investor, though. An S&P 500 ETF could accomplish similar exposure with less up-front capital.

Futures traders fall into two main groups: the hedgers and the speculators. The hedgers have an interest in the underlying commodity as a function of their core business. Hedgers seek to *hedge out*, or reduce the negative risk of price changes on their businesses such as agricultural farmers, oil refineries, and gold miners. And then there are the speculators, hedge fund types who seek to make a profit by predicting market moves, basically front-running the demand of the hedgers. Speculators buy (or sell) the commodity or financial future for which they have no practical use other than to sell (or buy) it at some later date at a profit.

Conclusion

One of the most powerful advantages of the hedge trader is virtual limitless access to financial instruments and contracts to express a market view. Basically, hedge fund managers will trade *anything* that can turn a profit for them. Sometimes it gets out of hand, like literally trading financial futures on the weather or trading exotic derivatives such as mortgage-backed securities that no one knows how to evaluate. Nonetheless, stocks, bonds, commodities, mutual funds, ETFs, and futures are all potential securities for you to consider when constructing your own strategies.

In the models herein, we are going to focus on equities and ETFs. The reason is that between common stocks and ETFs, you will be able to trade pretty much any investment idea you can think of. The ETFs are your secret weapon for leveling the playing field, because many of them achieve the same exposure as the big-money financial and commodities contracts and the options traded by the hedge funds. In no time you will be trading ideas like Gordon Gekko. You will see.

CHAPTER 2

OKAY, WHAT IS A HEDGE FUND?

Everyone is talking about hedge funds. We read about them in the newspapers, we hear about them on the financial news networks. And the context is usually a discussion of the enormous wealth generated by hedge fund managers for themselves and for their investors, the abysmal losses suffered by various funds (Amaranth Advisors, Long-Term Capital Management), or the outright fraud and subsequent collapse of some funds (Manhattan Investment Fund, Bayou Management). It seems that the hippest thing to be is a hedge fund trader. The once-hallowed jobs at investment banks are now considered as boring as the job of tax accountant. What's all the fuss about? What the hell is a hedge fund? And why should it matter to you?

Well, let's be honest. Most people have no idea what a true hedge fund is—including many of the people who actually run hedge funds! What we *do* know is that the guys who do it well make a lot of money. A whole *lot* of money. Just to give you an idea, one manager, Bruce Bovner,[1] is reputed to have personally made $700 million in 2006. How does that happen? With a management fee of 3 percent and total assets under management of over $15 billion, Bruce's fund makes

---

1. The name is changed.

$450 million just for getting out of bed. And 2006's salary wasn't anything new for Bruce: the year before, he (reputedly) earned $550 million. Over just those two years, he earned enough to buy an Apple MacBook for every adult in the United States.

Bruce is not alone, though. James Simons of Renaissance Technologies and T. Boone Pickens Jr. of BP Capital Management made $1.5 billion and $1.4 billion, respectively, in 2005. This kind of wealth creation boggles the mind and is one of the reasons hedge funds are so interesting. What's going on with these investment techniques to make that kind of money? And how can we get a piece of that action?

Background

Before we look at the details of what a hedge fund is, let us first go over some of the basics. Despite the media articles to the contrary, the original intent of the earliest hedge funds was to reduce the risk of investing directly in the market. Hedge funds were actually intended to be the *conservative* alternative to traditional investments. The technique was to hedge—reduce portfolio risk—the positions in one's portfolio and, as a result, minimize risk per unit of maximum potential gain.

In simple terms, to hedge is to buy or sell one security (or group of securities) with the objective to reduce the risk associated with a second security (or group of securities). The result is to simultaneously hold a collection of investment assets where some benefit in "up" markets and others benefit in "down" markets. Collectively, the held positions represent a hedge to one another, reducing risk while collectively remaining profitable as a portfolio. Bettors at the track do this all the time. They might place a small bet on a promising horse with little chance of winning but hedge that bet with a larger wager placed on the odds-on favorite. If well executed, the bettor should profit irrespective of which horse wins. Only the magnitude of the payout will change.

Alfred W. Jones and the Beginning of Hedge Fund Investing

An historical description of hedge funds must pay tribute to the father of hedge fund strategies, Alfred W. Jones. In 1949, Alfred Jones established the first hedge fund in the United States. At the time, hedging was a pioneering concept and a significant departure from the traditional way of investing. In contrast to the "buy-only" commingled investment vehicles available at the time, such as mutual funds, Jones offered a technique to his investors that sought to take advantage of market *declines* as well as market advances. Before that, investors sought only to buy attractive investments on the expectation of an *increase* in value, and they would simply avoid those investments that were expected to *decrease* in value.

Jones was the first to institute a strategy combining the practice of short selling (selling a security you do not yet own in order to buy it back at a lower price for a profit) with the traditional practice of purchasing stocks expected to increase in value. *The investment vehicle used to combine these two practices was known as a hedge fund.* The net result of the hedge technique was that it offered the opportunity for investors to profit in both up and down markets. To further enhance this double-profit opportunity, Jones borrowed capital from banks, secured by the fund's investment portfolio, in order to increase the size and therefore the profitability of each of the trades he executed.

As with any new enterprise, Jones needed to convince investors that hedging was a safe practice. Thus, Jones invested his own money in the fund, putting his own "skin" in the game. For that concession, Jones demanded a significant portion of the profits generated—20 percent—but his coinvestment ensured that he and his investors' goals were aligned.

These three innovations—short selling, using leverage, and manager participation in profits—distinguished the first hedge fund and continue to be the fundamental attributes of hedge funds today.

To my knowledge, none of the original funds that began in the late 1940s and early 1950s is still operating today. One of the reasons is that hedge funds are very closely associated with their founders, making it difficult for any fund to establish a legacy. Could you, for example, imagine anyone other than Warren Buffett running the Berkshire Hathaway fund?

Jones's Legacy

Hedge funds did not immediately catch on. There were a number of reasons for this. First the liquidity and leverage provided to hedge funds today wasn't possible way back when, so the eye-popping returns that have made hedge funds popular since the 1980s were rare in the beginning. It also takes time for innovation to catch on. We are all familiar with the S&P 500 Index, for example, but it took over twenty-five years for there to be any significant institutional capital commitment to trading an equity index.

With greater assets and the increased availability of leverage, hedge funds surged onto the landscape, taking advantage of opportunities in the markets in ways that, at that time, were novel and very profitable. Today, the techniques used by hedge fund managers in the 1980s would seem relatively ordinary; the techniques that "printed money" in the 1980s have less impact in today's evolved market.

The volatility of hedge fund returns in the 1980s was staggering, but so too were the total returns of the early masters. According to *Market Wizards* by Michael Marcus, one of the early masters, Bruce Kovner, had an average annual return of over 87 percent for the first ten years of operation, from 1982 to 1992. At the same time, the biggest peak-to-trough loss during that period was *more than 40 percent*! It was indeed a white-knuckle ride, but a very profitable one if you held on (screaming) for the full duration. And the ride made Kovner and his investors very, very wealthy.

Through hedging, a skillful manager can make profits regardless of whether the stock market advances or declines. So if the market collapses as it did in March 2000, if properly hedged, you could be one of the few who are left not only standing but smiling, too. I was fortunate to be one of the survivors and even a profiteer during the 2000 meltdown. During that time, half of my portfolio was short; I did not make much, but I did not lose either. The short hedges completely hedged my portfolio against losses.

At the time, my proposition was that I would return 1 percent per month, ostensibly "guaranteed" by an actively hedged portfolio. It was a proposition that sometimes got me laughed out of the room because during that period, the tech boom, potential investors guffawed that they made 1 percent or more every day. They weren't laughing when the market tanked, however, and the few who invested in our fund were delighted with a hedged return in 2000 of 11 percent for the year.

Today's hedge fund environment spans a far greater range of techniques than, say, Jones's early techniques, in part necessitated by an ever-learning and intelligent market. The advancement is a financial sort-of Moore's Law: fifty years ago, the computational power of computers that would fill entire floors now is contained in the chip inside a mobile phone. Hedge funds have had a similar maturation; today they range greatly in terms of the investment principles they employ. Some are more focused today on absolute uncorrelated return and others on leverage and direction.

Attempting to maximize profit to the fullest extent (call it "greed") has led to quite spectacular collapses in the modern era of hedge funds. For example, Amaranth's energy trades were volatile, but they had resulted in as much as 75 percent of Amaranth's profit in prior years.[2] One superstar trader generated almost all of Amaranth's return, and he was good at it . . . until he wasn't. His speculations in the energy markets resulted in losses of $6.5 billion over the course of just a few days. He literally put Amaranth out of business. His goal was to make as much money as he could, using essentially one methodology—market timing. It is, therefore, a misnomer to say that Amaranth was a hedge fund. There was no "hedge" about it. The problem was that Amaranth had oversize exposure to one return-generating engine. When that engine got in trouble, there was nothing to hedge the losses, which became exceptional in size and impact.

Simultaneous with the shift of focus to absolute return, the scope of tradable instruments for hedge funds has exploded. In chapter 1, we reviewed the universe of potential investment securities. Each security in that universe is a potential tool for the hedge fund manager. Truly, for every tradable security that exists globally, there is a hedge fund that trades it, particularly derivative instruments.[3] In some markets, such as

---

2. Amaranth Advisors LLC was an American multistrategy hedge fund managing US$9 billion in assets. In September 2006, it collapsed after losing roughly US$6 billion in a single week on natural gas futures. The failure was one of the greatest hedge fund collapses in history. [Wikipedia]

3. Derivatives are fancy, often complex, tradable securities whose value exists only in concept and is not necessarily tied to any tangible financial instrument. For example, an investor could buy a derivative that "bets" that interest rates will rise. There is no underlying instrument only a bet that a certain event will happen.

credit default swaps,[4] the size of the derivatives market is huge. JPMorgan alone held $92 trillion in derivative investments on its books in February 2008. That's $92 *trillion*. The magnitude of derivatives' dollar volume is precarious because, unlike a future, no money changes hands—just the differences in value exchange hands, like a future. The contract is secured with merely a pledge of collateral and very high leverage. JPMorgan was leveraged *74 to 1*. In some derivatives markets, there is more capital invested in the derivative bet than there is to safely satisfy all contracts. It is like leasing your car to ten people. Everything is fine as long as two or more of the lessees don't show up at the same time, expecting to use the car.

Enron traders were even making bets on the weather by using derivatives. If you had the financial resources, Enron was willing to make a market on whether or not it would be sunny tomorrow. Indeed, it suffices to say that hedge funds today trade a very wide range of instruments with a wide range of investment styles. It can sometimes get out of hand.

Why Not You?

To pull back the shroud of mystery that surrounds hedge funds, let us debunk one of the pervasive myths up front. **Hedge funds do not create any investment magic that you cannot create for yourself.** In fact, hedge funds attempt to do the same things you do: buy low and sell high.

A successful hedge fund strategy has three basic attributes:

1. **Investment Discipline:** This means developing a structured way of considering and acting on oppor-

---

4. A credit default swap is a swap in which one investor receives cash in return for guaranteeing to make a specific payment, should a negative credit event happen. One possible type of credit event is a downgrade in the credit status of a corporate entity.

tunities in the market. It is very important to have strong rules for entering a position and it is equally important—perhaps more important—to have strong rules for selling out of a position. By sticking to a structured discipline, the investor yields more predictable results.

2. **Creativity in Expressing Your Investment Views:** Find the right combination of tradable securities that reflects the risks and rewards you seek. If you believe that, say, rising energy prices will have an impact on the economy, you, the hedge fund manager, must determine what you can buy or sell that will position you to take advantage of this insight. Find the appropriate investments to express your view precisely.

3. **Evolve Your Strategy As Market Conditions Change:** Things change. Many a trader has bit the dust by sticking to a system that has already failed him. Conviction is an admirable personality trait in a friend, but when things are not working as planned, it is important to know when and how to move prudently and expeditiously to plan B.

There are some fundamental differences between you and the professional hedge fund manager. First of all, hedge fund managers spend a lot more time researching than you do, they have significantly more access to information resources than you do, and—perhaps—they are a bit more studied in mathematical finance.

Nonetheless, you do have a trove of resources available to you, too. Many financial information and research resources are free online. Information is power, and the more you have of it, the better. You would be surprised at how much improved your strategies would become if you developed your own ideas. Great ideas are freely available information gleaned from unbiased business periodicals. As one of my traders is fond of saying, Warren Buffett spends most of his day just reading and ingesting information. Find "adult" periodicals that report the news and avoid tabloid investment advice that is often worse than useless.

Probably the biggest secret with respect to achieving monster returns in hedge funds is the extent to which hedge funds have access to other people's money (OPM). OPM is one of the more significant advantages hedge managers have. If they raise sufficient capital, managers can get rich just by virtue of the sheer scale of the capital they control. Making a paltry 2 percent return on $100 million of assets under management (AUM) is nice. $2 million x the 20 percent incentive fee = $400,000 (yawn). Make the same paltry return on $10 billion of AUM, you'd have $40 million for the same year's toil. At some point, with scale, it is hard to lose as a hedge fund manager. The more successful managers charge even more, as much as a 4 percent management fee and a whopping 45 percent of profits.

The other source of OPM is leverage, or the practice of borrowing money to make bets. That may not seem like a big advantage, except that unlike the individual investor, who is limited to borrowing 50 percent of his account value (known as margin) to make an investment, hedge funds borrow up to 100 times or *10,000 percent* of their account value to make their bets.

In summary, hedge fund managers can take "intelligent" risks as a result of their access to a higher quality and quantity of information, they actively manage their market exposure; and they use OPM. You can express some of these features in your own portfolio.

Hedge Funds Described

Structurally, hedge funds are a type of mutual fund whose shares are available strictly by invitation. If you seek to purchase a regular mutual fund, you can find it through any broker—call your broker, and the next day it can be in your account. Mutual funds are regulated by the SEC, so there are restrictions on what they can do, which purportedly protects the investor from risk. Hedge funds are mutual funds without the rules. They are considered mutual because all investors commingle their funds in one account. Given that hedge funds are unregulated, you cannot simply call your broker to invest in one or even find data on their performance. Given that they are unregulated, it is against U.S. securities law for a hedge fund to advertise its performance or hold itself out to the general public.

Hedge funds represent the "velvet rope" of the investment community. Yes, you can be invited to the party, but the guest list is predicated on your having a bank balance of more than $5 million.[5] Few small investors can fill those shoes. But let's look at how, without being invited to these exclusive parties, you can create your own hedge fund–type investment opportunities.

Hedge funds are usually organized offshore to minimize tax implications for their investors and to minimize regulatory scrutiny, although that is slowly changing, as funds have voluntarily begun to register with the SEC. Some of the secrecy that surrounds them is in place to protect the efficacy of their investment ideas. And some of it is in place as a type of "client management"—a stiff-arm to those clients who would look over the shoulders of their managers or call too often.

---

5. As required by the SEC to invest in an unregulated fund. The standard is known as a Qualified Purchaser.

Hedge funds employ four basic techniques: 1. short selling; 2. leverage (borrowing money to increase the number of investments you can make); 3. diversity, making a wide range of investments; and, most important, 4. *hedging*!

I assure you that these are the only differences between a hedge fund and your own portfolio. Let's examine these points one at a time. We will reexamine these four techniques many times throughout this book.

Short Selling

Short selling is an extremely important tool in the hedge fund manager's tool kit. Short selling is, for example, how George Soros earned $1 billion *in one day* by betting on the demise of the British pound. In September 1992, Soros risked $10 billion on a single trade when he shorted the pound. The trade generated a profit of $1 billion, ultimately reaching $2 billion in profit in the days following. Short selling is also how Jim Chanos became a stock market legend with his short of Enron in late 2000. It turned out to be the short sell of the decade. Enron declined from a peak of $66 billion to $0 in a matter of days.

Many readers may know what short selling is or may even have shorted a stock, option, or future. But bear with me while I explain the concept and help you nail down the idea.

Let me start with a question. If you knew for certain that the price of a security was going to drop, what would you do? For example, what would you do today if you knew that IBM would decrease in value next week, and you didn't own any of the stock? Think about that for a second.

Martha Stewart could advise you what to do if you had advance knowledge of a stock's imminent decline if you *already* owned the stock. Ms. Stewart was allegedly tipped off that shares of ImClone (NASDAQ: IMCL) were going to decline. Since she already owned shares, she simply sold them. She sold based on a standing order to sell with her broker, which was put in place just prior to their precipitous decline in value. That's very straightforward. If you are convinced of an impending decline in value and you own shares, then you just sell. Easy. But that's not short selling.

What would you do if you knew that the shares of a company would decrease in value and you *didn't* own any shares? How would you profit? The answer is that you would sell the shares short.

A short is making a bet that the price of the security will decline by selling a security that *you do not own*. The objective is to buy it back at a lower price at a later date and make a profit. It is a "sell high, buy low" proposition for the investor, the opposite of the traditional "buy low, sell high" axiom— but it can be just as profitable. By selling a security short, you are literally borrowing it (usually from a bank or broker) at ostensibly no cost, and selling those borrowed shares in the market. The proceeds from the sale provide cash, just as if you had owned the shares, but it is balanced by the obligation to return the shares to the lender at some point in the future. You buy the shares back at a later date (hopefully at a lower price) so that you can return the borrowed shares to the stock lender and keep the cash difference. Since you receive cash for the sale of the securities, you are betting that the short-term performance of the cash will be better than the price appreciation/depreciation of the security. Oh, and you will receive market interest on the cash proceeds from selling the borrowed securities. Not bad, huh?

Let me give a simple metaphorical example. On Monday, you and only you find out that Bruce Springsteen has developed a sore throat in advance of a sold-out performance scheduled for the following Saturday. If you wanted to profit from this knowledge, what would you do?

First, of course, you would not tell a soul: great ideas are most profitable when they are in the hands of only a few. Then, you could offer your brother-in-law, Hank, $100 if he would be willing to let you hold (lend you) his two tickets until the morning of the show. Hank may think, "What a strange request," but given that he spent $1,000 to buy the tickets, he would be happy to reduce his overall ticket cost to $900. Hank hands over the tickets and gleefully collects your $100: *"Sucker!"* On Wednesday, ticket prices continue to rise in anticipation of the concert, so you sell the two tickets on craigslist for $1,200 to another would-be concertgoer.

Now you have $1,200 cash in your pocket, but that is not all profit, because you still owe the physical tickets back to Hank. On Thursday, it is announced that the concert is cancelled, and the cost of the tickets won't be refunded. For that reason, not only do ticket prices fall, but the tickets become worth less than face value. On Friday, you repurchase tickets for $0.10, about the cost of the paper they are printed on, and return the physical tickets to your hapless brother-in-law with a smile and a very sincere "thank you" on Saturday morning.

This set of transactions would not make you popular with Hank, but it would be a profitable strategy for capitalizing on bad news. You brought in $1,200 in cash against a cost of $100.10 ($100 to borrow the tickets; $0.10 to reacquire them) for a profit of $1,099.90—simply for taking advantage of information about which the rest of the world was in the dark.

Does this sound a little too easy? Of course it does. Our example is, unfortunately, a gross simplification, but it illustrates how to take advantage of insightful information regarding a potential *decline*.

The story does not always end so happily. Hank could have demanded his tickets back on Wednesday, forcing you to repurchase the tickets at market rate, which may have been greater than the price at which you had sold them. It is perfectly legal for the lender to demand his stock back at any time. Or Springsteen may have miraculously recovered, so the Thursday cancellation might never have materialized. In either of these cases, your short trade would have resulted in a loss. Moreover, in order to borrow the securities, you must also contribute collateral to the lending party, and yes, there is a charge to borrow. For securities that are readily available for the borrow (termed "liquid" securities), the costs are de minimus. But it occasionally happens that a few other people get the same short-sell idea. Such demand reduces the number of shares that are available to borrow and thereby increases the borrowing cost. The resultant borrow costs can be great indeed.

Let's now examine a real-life example. Do you know Jim Chanos? He is a successful, dedicated short seller who had a strong conviction that Enron's stock price was significantly overvalued in 2001. So what did he do? He did what you did in the example above. He borrowed millions of shares of Enron from banking institutions and broker/dealers. He promised to give the shares back one day. Then he sold those shares to investors who (shall we say mistakenly) remained bullish on Enron stock. When all hell broke loose, as Enron shares traded to significantly lower levels, Chanos bought back the stock for pennies on the dollar and, in the process, generated significant profits for his investors.

Below is an historical chart of Enron's stock price, which makes clear why short selling can be very profitable when you know what you are doing. According to Chanos, he began shorting Enron in November 2000 when the share price was in the 50s and 60s. He probably experienced a bit of pain as Enron's price continued to climb after his trade, to as high as $90 per share, but in the end it was a maximally profitable short sale.

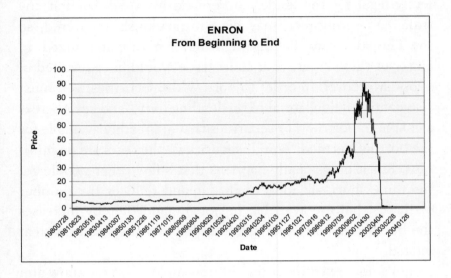

Some of the shrewdest investors are short sellers. Accounting irregularities, hidden partnerships, and earnings manipulation all create ripe opportunities for short sellers to take advantage of an impending deflation in a stock's trading price. Think of short sellers as being veteran accounting sleuths, assiduously combing through publicly available company data. These sleuths can pick up subtle warning signs and see through corporate spin with forensic clarity. And they know how to quiz accomplices and witnesses to put together the whole story, detail by detail.[6] They keep searching until they find a company that is weak enough to justify seeking profits from a short sale.

According to Chanos, short selling is a great opportunity

---

6. George Anders, "How to Find the Next Enron," *Fast Company* magazine.

when "companies appear to have materially overstated earnings, been victims of a flawed business plan, or been engaged in outright fraud." Below is an excerpt of Jim Chanos' testimony before congressional representatives investigating the Enron collapse:

My involvement with Enron began normally enough. In October of 2000, a friend asked me if I had seen an interesting article in the *Texas Wall Street Journal* (a regional edition) about accounting practices at large energy trading firms. The article, written by Jonathan Weil, pointed out that many of these firms, including Enron, employed the so-called "gain-on-sale" accounting method for their long-term energy trades. Basically, "gain-on-sale" accounting allows a company to estimate the future profitability of a trade made today, and book a profit today based on the present value of those estimated future profits.

Our interest in Enron and the other energy trading companies was piqued because our experience with companies that have used this accounting method has been that management's temptation to be overly aggressive in making assumptions about the future was too great for them to ignore. In effect, "earnings" could be created out of thin air if management was willing to "push the envelope" by using highly favorable assumptions. However, if these future assumptions did not come to pass, previously booked "earnings" would have to be adjusted downward. If this happened, as it often did, companies addicted to the crack cocaine of "gain-on-sale" accounting would simply do new and bigger deals (with a larger immediate "earnings" impact) to offset those downward revisions. Once a company got on such an accounting treadmill, it was hard for it to get off.

Chanos' success should not suggest that all short-sell trades are profitable. On the contrary, given that markets generally trend up as the economy grows, the majority of short-sell trades lose money. In fact, short sellers often have long streaks of unprofitable years as the markets advance, only to make a killing when the markets "correct downward." Being on the wrong side of a short position in bull markets can be painful indeed. When Chanos shorted the stock, it continued to rise for some period, by as much as 50 percent. Chanos therefore lost money initially. Loss is limitless with short sales, theoretically, because there is no ceiling on how high a stock can go. All the while, each tick in the wrong direction means more loss for the short "investment." Had that happened with Enron, Chanos would have had to buy back the stock at a higher price in order to stem his losses.

Since stock values are limited on the downside (no stocks have a value less than zero) and are unlimited on the upside (there is no upper limit to the price of a stock theoretically), the errant short sale can result in a loss that exceeds the initial investment. Such a prospect is known as a short squeeze. If you short a stock and it subsequently triples, you would lose two times, or 200 percent of your original investment. Ouch. Conversely, the maximum that a short position can return is 100 percent. It can only go to zero.

Leverage and "Other People's Money" (OPM)

Did you know that when Bear Stearns failed that some of its trade positions exceeded *100 to 1* leverage? "Leverage" just means that Bear borrowed money to make its investments. And it means that for every $1 Bear invested in a security, it was able to invest $99 more using OPM. That may seem crazy, but such leverage is not so uncommon among the banks and hedge funds.

Think about that proposition with respect your own portfolio. Can you imagine that your broker would allow you to invest a hundred times your deposit? Your $10,000 account would suddenly be trading $1 million of securities. That is a lot of money! Used prudently, such leverage can deliver impressive gains. The horror is that your account would be secured only by the $10,000 cash. A 1 percent loss on the *notional* $1 million would result in wiping out the entire $10,000 cash collateral. At that point—probably well before—your broker would liquidate your account in order to recover the loan he gave you or the $990,000 that was left, otherwise known as a margin call. In the case of Bear, it had billions of market positions and trillions of derivative products all aggressively leveraged. Can you see how a slight tumble in prices could bring down the entire market like cascading dominos? Can you imagine the impact of a margin call on Bear, forcing the sale of such a large portfolio of securities in the financial markets? The congressional jury is still out regarding the Fed's action, but I give "thumbs up" to the Fed for taking strong action and averting what could have been a veritable catastrophe.

Compare a leveraged position to an unleveraged position. Let's say you invested $10,000 in Google at the beginning, from the initial public offering (IPO) in August 2004, at $85 per share. Had you participated in the IPO, you would probably have been very happy with Google's peak value of $740 in November 2007, which would have given you a total return of 870 percent in just four years. $87,000. Not bad. Now imagine if you had access to 100 to 1 leverage to make the same trade. Your $10,000 investment would have become $8,700,000 during the same period, which would have made you *really* happy.

Make no mistake about it—leverage is a key element in

the profitability of hedge funds. This is especially true today, as the drive for returns has intensified and the fat, obvious opportunities have significantly declined due to the sheer magnitude of speculative capital. Market opportunities are increasingly less profitable for the same risk, adding leverage to these market opportunities enhances profits, so leverage has become very popular amongst hedge funds. Some critics claim that it is the *only* reason hedge funds outperform their traditional long-only counterparts. But like it or not, overall, leverage remains the single most important factor in the generation of hedge fund profits.

The big boys are able to get leverage that is generally unavailable to the average investor. If you are an ordinary investor, you can probably get only 1.5 times leverage. Average individuals do not have the same access to leverage as the big players because their accounts are not of sufficient size for their brokers to actually pay attention to them. But individual investors can access leverage in other ways. Leverage is available, for example, through some investment instruments by default, such as options or futures. Futures generally have 20 to 1 leverage built right in. In other words, you would only have to put up $5 of capital for every $100 of investment. With options, the inherent leverage is 100 to 1. For every one share of an option represents a hundred shares of the underlying security. And there are ETFs, like Ultra Dow30 ProShares (DDM), that provide 2 times leverage. Leverage is available to the average investor—but please, use it with caution!

What traders forget from time to time is that leverage cuts both ways. Leverage can increase your profits, but it can also multiply your losses. Let's look at an example using 100 to 1 leverage for the average investor and examine the consequence of profit or loss. The investor deposits $1,000 and the broker "loans" him $99,000 for one month at an annual rate of 6 percent interest. Let's assume that the investor puts all of the money, $100,000, in IBM. If IBM advances 10 percent, then the investor makes a $10,000 profit on a $1,000 investment, for a whopping 1,000 percent return. Nice! But if IBM declines by 10 percent, the investor loses not only all of his initial investment of $1,000 *but also has to pay the broker an additional $9,000 in losses.* In the latter case, the investor loses *more* than his original investment due to leverage. In reality, the broker would have closed the account long before such losses were realized, but it does illustrate that leverage is only great when your position is winning. Even if the price of IBM had stayed the same, the investor would have lost money due to the cost of borrowing the money for one month ($495).

Investment Universe

In the last chapter, we spoke of the potential instruments in which the do-it-yourself investor could invest: stocks, bonds, ETFs, and commodities. Your investment universe will be one of the most important choices you will make in devising your own hedge strategy. There is no ideal universe of instruments to consider. It all depends on what you can handle in terms of research and data. Some hedge fund managers trade as few as twelve to fifteen stocks *total*, but they know those companies really, really well. Other funds, like global macro funds, trade in virtually any instrument that trends, from cattle futures to global currencies. As long as a trend or profit potential exists, any financial instrument is a potential profit maker.

Personally, I have always selected an equity universe that is highly liquid, is well covered by Wall Street analysts, and for which market data is readily available. I have never sought out the "gems in the rough"—small-capitalization companies that no one has ever heard of. That is the right decision for me, while I acknowledge that there are many skillful and successful investors in small-cap stocks who do quite well. But for my skill set, "pairs trades" (i.e., buying one stock and short selling another "like" stock as a hedge against it) are the right fit. When I select well, the stocks I have purchased outperform the stocks I have shorted under all market circumstances, and I make a hedge profit. I trade, moreover, all large-cap companies that could withstand a large investment—tens of millions—without moving the market.[7]

For new investors, it is safest to start with a universe that you know well, perhaps the industry in which you work. If you know your job and your company, you are likely to know how your company, its competitors, and the industry as a whole is performing. As your expertise and confidence grows, you can expand your universe to include other industries and asset classes.

Overall, the investment universe of hedge funds has significantly expanded over the years. Hedge funds are now in private equity (investing in private companies that are not yet publicly traded), long-only equity (buying stocks long, only with no hedge), credit default swaps (a "bet" with a counterparty on whether a company will default), single-sector strategies (such as energy-only funds), and more. Multistrategy hedge funds have a diversified investment universe, important because it means that they do not have to rely on one source of return. The overall portfolio generates returns consistently and minimizes fluctuations by virtue of having several value drivers. Diversification in your investment universe will generally reduce risk and stabilize your portfolio returns, as well.

---

7. Meaning that the price of the stock will not move as a result of my trades. Highly liquid securities can take a higher volume of trades from one investor without those trades affecting the stock price.

Hedging

Hedging is the most important part of your hedge strategy. It sounds obvious, but in practice it is not. Anyone can invest in a bull market and make money. My nephew made money in the run-up in the equity markets to 2000. He is six years old. But he would not have performed as well in a downtrending or sideways market. A hedge strategy should remain profitable and be protected from unanticipated market turns by having exposure on both sides of the market. Let me give a visual example.

Take a look at the stock chart below. It is a six-month price history of Google, from March to September of 2006. It looks like a pretty volatile investment. It *is* volatile; during this six-month span, Google's stock price bounced between $360 and $440 five times, a total cumulative movement of more than 100 percent of the total value: up (22 percent), down (20 percent), up, down, each time cycling 50 percent in value mileage. If you held on to Google during this six-month period you would have made money (from $360 to a final value of $408, for a 13 percent return), but you would have had a wild, gut-twisting ride.

In hindsight, it is convenient to observe that one would have held on to the stock given such gyrations, but I can tell you from experience, when you are in the trenches, those seemingly innocuous turns in the graph add up to quite uncomfortable fluctuations in your account. It can be very difficult to hold a position as you watch your losses accumulate. You might need a good stash of Prilosec.

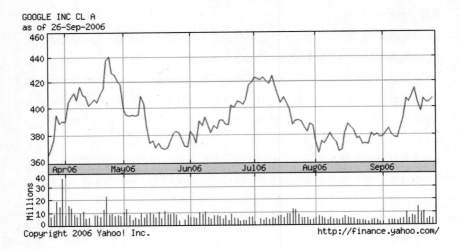

GOOGLE INC CL A
as of 26-Sep-2006

Copyright 2006 Yahoo! Inc.   http://finance.yahoo.com/

Google is obviously a very strong company and a very good long-term buy. But holding Google in your portfolio during that period would have been a nerve-wracking experience. Depending on where you bought in, you could now and again have been significantly underwater, and yet it was still a great long-term hold. If you bought in at $440, though, you wouldn't have been too happy when it hit $370, a 16 percent loss. There is a lot of volatility there, and volatility is the by-product of a buy-and-hold position. Wouldn't it be better to have achieved the same 13 percent return without the daily and weekly fluctuations in asset value?

So you have a choice: invest in a security and hold on for the ride, or find a way to hedge your investment, eliminating some of the volatility while still holding the security long term. We have already learned about short selling. What would be the effect if you sold short a security that had "like" market characteristics but over time underperformed the stock you were interested in? Yahoo!, the stock below, is in the same investment category as Google: Technology. Given that these stocks are in the same industry, they have many of the same performance characteristics market risks. Therefore they may make a reasonable hedge.

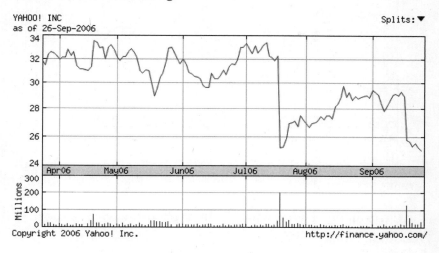

YAHOO! INC
as of 26-Sep-2006
Splits: ▼

Copyright 2006 Yahoo! Inc. http://finance.yahoo.com/

Yahoo!'s performance looks very similar to that of Google, except one important difference: the return performance over the same observation period is less than that of Google. In fact, Yahoo! returned a lot less than Google, at *minus* 20 percent. So as a hedge, one might buy Google and short sell Yahoo! to reduce market risk while generating returns that are independent of the market. Let's examine it. On the following page is a graph of an investor's performance if he had bought Google and shorted Yahoo!

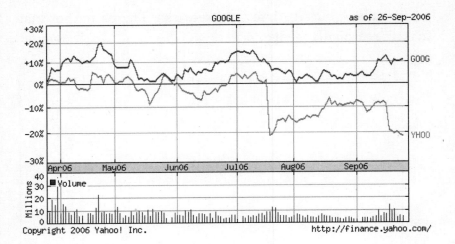

If you hedged your Google long position with a short in Yahoo! in equal dollar amounts, it would have returned 30 percent over the six-month period versus only 10 percent for the Google-only long position. On a hedge comprised of $10,000 long in Google and $10,000 short in Yahoo!, at the end of the period, the Google long would have returned roughly 10 percent ($1,000) and the Yahoo! short would have returned 20 percent ($2,000). The distance between the end points of those two stocks on the graph is your profit. And note that since the short sale generates cash, it costs only $10,000 to invest $10,000 long and $10,000 short. This hedge generated a total profit of $3,000 on a cash cost of $10,000, for a total 30 percent return on capital with a very low risk profile.

It doesn't always work out that way, of course. Yahoo! may have outperformed Google, and you would have lost money. Or perhaps Yahoo! may have returned 6 percent over the same period, so your hedge position would have returned you only 4 percent versus the 13 percent you would have earned by holding Google only . . . and so on. The point is that by taking a hedge position, you can significantly reduce your risk of holding a single position. The Google (long) and Yahoo! (short) position is known as a pairs trade, where the investor wishes to benefit from his expectation that one security will perform better than another while hedging out market risk. The best pairs are those in the same or similar industries or ones where one industry has a clear advantage over the other, such as buying wireless phone carriers and selling wireline phone companies against them as a hedge.

As noted earlier, hedging and hedge strategies are specifically intended to *reduce* risk by hedging one's exposures. Hedging is a technique that seeks profit by buying a "long" position while reducing the investor's overall risk exposure by hedging, selling, against it. The hedge position may return more or less return than would holding the long security outright. It will depend on the relative performance of the "legs" of the hedge. If the short outperforms the long, then the hedge would generate a loss. The idea is to have a hedge portfolio of a dozen or more pairs trades that are similarly contrived to profit from the relative performance between two securities. If you have, say, twenty pairs trades in your portfolio, not all of the pairs will be profitable, but your portfolio will be significantly less volatile. And if, overall, you have chosen your pairs carefully, you might even make some profit.

Why does a pairs trade work? Well, approximately 85 percent of stock-price changes are a result of movements in the general market and not anything specific about the company.[8] In other words, if a long stock position you have purchased

---

8. Specific risk is the risk associated with individual assets. Within a portfolio, these risks can be reduced through diversification, i.e., specific risks "cancel out." Specific risk is also called diversifiable, unique, unsystemic, or idiosyncratic risk. Systemic risk (aka portfolio risk or market risk) refers to the risk common to all securities. Except for selling short, systemic risk cannot be diversified away (within one market). Within the market portfolio, asset specific risk will be diversified away. Systemic risk is therefore equated with the risk (standard deviation) of the market portfolio.

advances up in direction, on average, its advance can be explained by the advance of the market itself. The overall market, therefore, would be responsible for 85 percent of a stock's advancement. The other 15 percent of stock movements is based upon attributes specific to the company. If a company is executing its operating plan or growth strategy well, its stock price may outperform the market return or, more important, outperform its peers (such as Google outperformed Yahoo! in the period we examined).

What you want to do is short a stock that has a profile similar to the long choice but whose management execution or competitive and strategic positioning—the marginal 15 percent, is such that you believe it will underperform your long stock. This is known as a beta neutral or market neutral hedge.

In practice, it is not so easy. Today, with the proliferation of long/short strategies, statistical arbitrage,[9] and other such players in the markets, many of the obvious ideas have been picked over, so choose carefully. During a rising market, good long stocks rise more than the market, while good short stocks rise less than the market. In a declining market, good long selections decline less than the market, and good short selections decline more than the market, yielding a net profit in all market conditions. An investor applying this technique would be in a position to achieve positive returns irrespective of market direction and would be thus hedged to the market. There are many eyes on these types of trades, however, increasingly making pairs selection a challenge.

---

9. Statistical arbitrage strategies trade against a price breakout of a stock using mathematical signals. If a stock has a move that is unwarranted relative to its peers, statistical arbitrageurs will trade to bring it back in line, profitably.

Directional Bets

Hedge fund critics crow that hedge funds are simply lever-aged mutual funds. They suggest that hedge funds exploit the same-old long-only opportunities that ordinary mutual funds do, then enhance the return by applying leverage. In some cases, that is true. Many hedge fund strategies are dependent on pure market direction (usually up) and are thus directional bets. Not all hedge funds seek to be market or beta neutral. Some make directional bets *with* the market by design, believ-ing that they can time a market's change in direction better than other investors.

Strategies such as global macro are particularly directional, seeking to capture macro trends ("the trend is your friend" trades). Managers using these strategies identify as many trad-able trends as they can—in interest rates, commodity prices, equity indices, etc—and structure a portfolio of multiple di-rectional bets to capture them. Though their investments are not classically hedged, the sum total of their investments (the-oretically) diversifies their risk such that the performance of the collective portfolio is not highly correlated to the general markets. Nonetheless the Sharpe Ratios (a statistical measure of the quality of strategy's return) of directional strategies are often low. A Sharpe Ratio, the portfolio return divided by the variability of the return, greater than 1 is very good. It means that taking the risk of making your investment is better than holding cash, even when the returns of the risky investment have been adjusted for the risk taken. A ratio of less than 1 suggests that you are better off buying CDs than making the investment being considered. Nonetheless, there are some trend players who do quite well year after year, while over time, their Sharpe Ratios fluctuate greatly.

Directional hedge fund managers avoid concentrated ex-posure to any one market, but when a trend is strong, they can pile on to the trend with great results. For example, in the last two quarters of 2006, the European markets were on fire. From August 2006 through December 2006, the German stock market, represented by the DAX 30, returned 26 percent from a low of 5300 in June to a high of 5600 in December. Global directional traders piled onto this advance, with leverage, and made a fortune. Even in an individual's brokerage account—with only 1.5 to 1 leverage—that's a 40 percent return in six months. Pretty good. In a strongly trading market, a trader would always do better buying direction without the hedge. When the trend is strong, hedge traders don't fight it, they ride it.

This does not hold true only for equities. From January 2006 to January 2007, NYMEX crude oil futures went from a high of 78 to a low of 50—a loss of 36 percent—putting some funds out of business that expected a rebound in the "black gold." Of course, if you had shorted the trend, you would have *profited* 36 percent. The trend is best when it is on your side. And trends cut both ways. Crude oil subsequently "trended" over several months to a stunning high of $145. Lots of the same traders participated in this move/trend, with mixed results for the economy.

Arbitrage

Arbitrage is likely the least volatile of all hedge strategies, but in practice it is rare, inasmuch as the market is sufficiently competitive that true arbitrage has largely been driven out. Arbitrage involves the simultaneous buying and selling of a security at two different prices in two different markets, resulting in profits *without risk.*

Perfectly efficient markets generally do not present arbitrage opportunities, so today, pure arbitrage is either rare or certainly not widely known; strategists aware of a pure arbitrage opportunity have a great incentive to keep such knowledge to themselves. Here is an example of structural arbitrage, assuming unlimited demand. The price of a container of lemonade on Manhattan's Lower East Side (LES) is $8, and it is selling for $11 on Manhattan's Upper West Side (UWS). There is a $2 per container cost for transportation. Assuming that demand meets supply, an arbitrageur buying on the LES and simultaneously selling on the UWS would generate a riskless profit of $1.00 per container. The more transactions you do, the more money you will make. Without risk.

Arbitrage opportunities do not stick around for long, however. The knowledge of an arbitrage seeps into the intelligence of the market, and others begin to see and trade the same idea, making it less profitable over time and perhaps even a losing trade. In index arbitrage, for example, the manager takes advantage of mispricings between index futures[10] and the underlying stocks. Years ago, index arbitrage strategies used to be a significantly profitable cash cow for the proprietary trading desks at investment banks. Today, there are sufficient numbers of traders monitoring and seeking to profit from this mispricing that the reward for identifying the mispricing is no longer robust; the profit narrows and no longer exceeds the price of execution. Thus, the opportunity was "arbed out." For every market opportunity, the market has a learning curve, chipping away at the opportunity until marginal profit equals marginal cost.

---

10. A futures contract on a stock or financial index. The S&P 500 Index is one of the most widely traded index futures contracts in the United States. Occasionally the calculated price of the future does not equal the sum of the value of its constituents, presenting an arbitrage opportunity. Such mispricings are increasingly rare.

Generating Trade Ideas

Every day my inbox is brimming with investment "ideas" pushed by investment banks and various "analysts" and researchers. I generally ignore them because, for the most part, once an idea has gone into print, it has diminished in value. If someone is selling a trade idea, he, like any salesman, is selling to as many buyers as he can. By the time I have heard of an idea, it is already stale bread. This is why I will not attempt to provide you with specific trading ideas. They would be old by the time you read them. We will focus on process instead.

Good research and great ideas will be the biggest challenge for you. The "best" ideas are sometimes so picked over that they represent more risk than opportunity. The entrance door to a great investment idea is wide and tall when an investment is performing as expected (i.e., profitably), but the exit doors are as small as a thumbnail when things go wrong resulting in precipitious declines. Supply-and-demand dynamics would dictate that when the proverbial "dookey" hits the fan, investors clamor for the exits, and, like musical chairs, the last to leave a position get burned. A well-known example of this (besides the famed tulip bulb craze in Holland in 1630) is the technology bubble in the United States. There was a wide-open door as buyers both large and small entered the U.S. technology market. But when it became clear that the pricing for technology shares was grossly inflated, every investor ran for the exits, and the market collapsed. When the market reacts en masse to negative news, security prices fall precipitously. The peak to trough sell-off from the burst of the tech bubble was −45 percent. Technology buys were a great idea, but once share prices exceeded reasonable levels, shares plummeted.

It is important for you to cultivate your own fresh research and ideas. I believe that great investment themes can be expertly produced and executed on your own. That means reading the ideas of others that are public and forming your own opinion. Every investor is an expert at something. My mother is a prodigious but thrifty shopper. That practice gives her insights into the growth prospects of discount retailers: retailers that offer better bang per buck may have higher long-term growth potential. Just look at Wal-Mart.

Last year, one of my friends remarked that the limousines outside of Lehman Brothers were lined up down the block late in the evening, day after day. This suggested to him that they were doing deals—lots of deals. Indeed, Lehman stock was up 23 percent in 2006. (Turns out that was a bubble too, though. Lehman was bankrupt and out of business by September 2008.)

Another friend is a real estate developer, which potentially gives him specific insight into stocks that are dependent on real estate values, such as REITS (real estate investment trusts). Do not be afraid to trade on the expertise you already have. Chances are you know from your own personal experiences as much or more than any analyst about *your* profession. A little bit further along, I will show you how to formulate those ideas into a hedged investment strategy.

Conclusion

A hedge fund is a lot of things, but it has the basic characteristics of seeking returns that are uncorrelated with full market risk. This is accomplished through four fundamental investment techniques, including primarily 1. short selling; 2. leverage; 3. creativity combined with a wide range of investment types; and, most important, 4. *hedging!*

CHAPTER 3

WHY HEDGE FUNDS MATTER

The reputation of hedge funds varies. The associations that most often come to mind for the average person when they think "hedge fund" are "great risk" and "great greed." Traditional long-only investors, because they have achieved success without using the leverage, high turnover, risk management, and the compensation structure associated with hedge funds, have long been critical of hedge funds. Some have presciently forecast the collapse of the hedge fund industry due to its folly of rewarding the cowboy mentality. However, the din of such opinions has been on the decline as the techniques of hedge funds have proven themselves through superior risk-adjusted performance over the years.

I recall an early article about hedge funds written by a prominent analyst who, ten years ago, derided the industry as little more than a highly profitable "compensation scheme [for its managers] masquerading as an asset class." This critique pointed out that the compensation structure of hedge funds rewarded risky behavior by encouraging traders to swing for the fences. The suggestion was that the business structure was flawed because it impels high-risk behavior to the detriment of a hedge fund's investors, and perhaps the entire market.

The worst side of that sentiment is that if the trading does not work out, some managers can choose to toss in the keys and just walk away. The high-water mark on performance makes it more likely that a manager would toss in the keys if the fund's performance becomes negative. It does happen. In that case, managers believe it's better to walk away, return capital, and start over. It is the incentive fee, the 20 percent of profits, that gets hedge managers' knickers in a twist. Without substantial profits, a hedge fund does not pay out to the manager much more than a traditional mutual fund does.

The analyst's point has some merit. I have personally witnessed more than one instance of a manager's proverbial key-toss and subsequent self-reinvention. But years later the same analyst, now a partner in a hedge fund himself, argued in a Webcast to his clients that the industry has mistakenly rewarded hedge fund managers for *minimizing* risk; managers, he argued, should be rewarded for taking more risk than the general market—albeit intelligent risk. Quite a turnaround. Perhaps specious. But I agree.

The Cost of Doing Business

The industry as a whole is brutally Darwinian. Hedge funds fail or evolve for a variety of reasons, but the prospect of success boils down to management's ability to attract and retain investment capital. From the jump, the business structure of a hedge fund makes it difficult to succeed. The reason is that the guys who know how to consistently make money in the markets demand big dough for their market savvy. A hedge fund manager who decides to open a fund with just two analysts has a personnel cost of at least $3 million ($1 million per head) if the analysts are good. Given that most hedge funds have a 1 percent or 2 percent management fee, that would mean that the founder would have to raise at least $100 million right out of the gate just to break even on personnel costs.

The founder may get a boost if he is coming from a pedigree hedge fund with a strong track record, but the average hedge fund debuts with less than $50 million under management. The fund is already starting behind the game.

Even before the first trade, the clock is ticking. The fund can pay its sages less than market, but then again, you get what you pay for. What's more, the fund needs to hit some early home runs in order to stimulate asset growth and investor interest. The typical fund takes 20 percent of profits, but it generally also has a high-water mark—meaning that the manager can take a share of profits only from the point of highest cumulative return. Any losses must be regained before the manager can take a share of profits. If the fund starts out with a weak year or a weak quarter, the combined prospect of weak interest from would-be investors plus the prospect of having to regain an historical loss prior to participating again in the profits, a savvy manager may be compelled to return the capital and start all over again. If at first you don't succeed . . .

Investment capital in hedge funds is impatient for performance, especially for young funds. There are lots of articles about the explosion of capital into the hedge fund industry. Less reported are the hundreds or thousands of funds that go out of business each year, out of a universe of nine thousand hedge funds. Each new fund must swiftly prove that it is a profitable, sustainable alternative or it is doomed. Only the strong survive—and even some of the strong performers do not survive if they cannot attract sufficient assets to sustain. It is thus an industry where the assets are fairly concentrated: three hundred funds control 70 percent of the $1.4 trillion in assets.

Hedge funds are far more than a compensation scheme for its managers, but the compensation impels a better "product." For any business, compensation schemes are the single most important tool for getting the best out of its human capital, whether that compensation is financial or something else (long vacations, creative freedom, etc.). The opportunity to participate in the performance of the fund helps to attract and retain the best managers. That, and the prospect of amassing true wealth in a relatively short period of time. The incentive fee structure is analogous to employees owning the stock of the company at which they are employed. Because of stock ownership, managers work longer and jump higher. Statistics show that young hedge funds systematically outperform their mature counterparts by an average of nearly 5 percent per year. New managers, eager to establish themselves as winners, simply work harder at sniffing out market opportunities. Few people are familiar with fifteen- to twenty-hour workdays, seven days a week, but they are not atypical for the driven in hedge funds.

In the early days, when I was setting up my first clients, I practically did not sleep for more than a month. I was so driven that I did not concern myself with sleep. Moreover, I could not have slept even if I had wanted to—I was too excited. One morning during this sleepless period I awoke[1] to find that I had gone completely blind in my right eye due to acute stress. I remember thinking to myself, "I don't care. If that's the price to pay to succeed at this, then I will pay the price. I will just use one eye."[2] I later learned from my doctor that it was the worst case of central serous retinopathy that he had ever seen in his career.

In Defense of Hedge Funds

The result of commingling driven minds and copious resources is that hedge funds play a significant role in creating wealth for their investors while providing the service of

---

1. Okay, so some nights I slept a little.
2. It eventually reverted.

liquidity to the capital markets. The nimbleness, size, and intelligence with which the hedge funds allocate capital keep the markets honest and moving toward "greater" efficiency. Capital flows into areas of highest payout per unit of risk, which results in the development of promising nascent companies or the elimination of profligate laggards. What that means to you, or to the man on Main Street, is that capital is being deployed to its highest and best use. Companies that should fail are forced to fail. Companies that are undervalued relative to their potential growth are invested in, or they are acquired. The resulting upside for the average bystander is economic benefit.

Efficient capital movement creates jobs and lowers production costs and therefore increases productivity. As of this writing, the dollar is in the basement, making it expensive for Americans to travel abroad to enjoy the beaches of Barcelona or a shopping spree in London. Hell, even Montreal is expensive right now. Hedge funds are not entirely responsible for the decline, but speculative capital is. It is controversial but when American companies with a global reach had to decide whether to manufacture locally for $10 when they could manufacture abroad for $1, the decision was clear: manufacture the products overseas and ship them back. Capital found its way to the most efficient engine for production. Globally, more jobs were created than lost, though that did not bode well for the displaced worker in Ohio. In order to compete, the U.S. did not lower prices explicitly but the dollar's value has plummeted relative to other currencies. There is a benefit too: the low value of the dollar was probably the only thing that is now keeping the U.S. out of a recession. Exports represent about 30 percent of the economy, and exports are booming. That was some silver lining to the man on main Street.

Or how about companies that have directly benefited from

the attention of hedge fund managers? Investor Carl Icahn, an activist hedge fund manager, has significantly enhanced equity value by being a proactive investor. The increase in value is known as the Icahn Lift. The saying (attributable to Carl Icahn of course) goes: "If you are invested in the market, then Carl Icahn has, most likely, helped improve your portfolio value." The Icahn Lift is the uptick in value that occurs when he has accumulated a position in a company, usually because he believes it is undervalued or poorly run. Icahn claims he has enriched investors by $55 billion, but this does not take into account the ancillary effects on other companies in which he is not invested but that are influenced by his activity. To be sure, Carl Icahn is only one of hundreds of activist investors. Collectively nonetheless they are value creators. That also benefits the man on Main Street.

Dynamic capital allocation raises ambient wealth through the market's implicit allocation of capital where it is best utilized, and hedge funds are central drivers of such movements. Why else would a company seek to globalize its reach if not to create a higher rate of return for its investors? Why would a company be concerned about margins, efficient use of capital, or the buying power of its own equity if not for the financial policemen who are looking over its shoulder? If capital invested in companies were apathetic and year-over-year performance unimportant, companies would naturally languish. This is a real phenomenon. When West Germany absorbed East Germany, for example, East German factories were not only worthless; they had negative value because the cost to make them competitive exceeded the cost of building new factories from scratch. Communism didn't force the efficient deployment of capital or reward the efficient use of resources as would a capitalist system. There was neither carrot nor stick.

But examples of inefficient capital deployment still abound in the domestic markets:

> Twenty-five years ago, G.M.'s share of the U.S. market was over 50 percent. Ten years ago, they had 33 percent, and today they have just 25 percent. G.M. is not alone: In 1991, Detroit's big three held almost 71 percent of the U.S. market; now they have just 58 percent, and that number shows no signs of changing direction. Indeed, Chrysler is basically out of business, and Ford is looking shaky at best. How did three of the world's most recognizable brand names become dinosaurs on the brink of extinction? What happened?
>
> A complacent arrogance on the part of the U.S. automakers' management is largely to blame. Years ago, people went to work for G.M., Ford and Chrysler because they were great, cushy jobs. You didn't have to do a darn thing, and as long as you showed up and kept your nose clean, eventually you could buy a nice pile in Grosse Pointe or Bloomfield Hills. The problem was, these coddled executives eventually became upper management, and snoozed their way through the 1980s and 1990s as the foreign auto makers blew right by them.[3]

Contrast GM with Toyota: today GM is worth about $5 billion, while Toyota is worth $160 billion. Forty years ago it was ostensibly the reverse.

The fact that there are smart people foraging the capital markets for hidden mispricing or capital opportunity means that capital is always flowing to the best and most efficient destinations. This is not to say that hedge funds create a bed of roses. Hedge funds have been known to cause huge disruptions and market bubbles, too. Market bubbles occur when

---

3. "Can General Motors Survive?" *The New York Observer*, March 27, 2005.

exuberance is not tempered by common sense. On occasion, hedge investors buy solely for the prospect of benefiting from trends while ignoring the fundamentals. The real estate bubble seems silly now: lenders provided loans to people who had poor credit, put no money down, and agreed to usurious interest-rate increases at some later date because they believed they could borrow *even more* from the target property through a home equity loan. Huh? But the fees were fat, real estate prices continued to rise, and hedge funds snapped up the loans because the yield was delicious. It made no sense but the ride was printing money, until it blew up.

Still, market bubbles occurred long before the existence of hedge funds. For the most part, hedge funds enable the markets to redeploy capital quickly and efficiently because they are not limited by the restrictions of regulated funds. Mutual funds, for example, usually have a strict mandate for the scope of their investing (if, say, they are large-cap U.S. funds, they cannot buy energy IPOs from Brazil). Collectively, hedge funds have a mandate to invest in any and all opportunities, and as a result, opportunities are more open. Such liquidity is both the burn and the salve. In 1998, when Long-Term Capital Management (LTCM) failed, it was due to an illiquidity, a potential loss, of about $4.4 billion, and it almost brought the *world* to its knees, with the credit markets screeching to a halt. Today, though I do not trivialize the problem of the mortgage market—we have written down *more than $500 billion* in bad investments in mortgages. There are estimates that when all is said and done, financial institutions may have written off as much as $1 trillion in bad debts. And so far the "experts" are not even sure whether there will be a U.S. recession. That is a huge difference in just ten years.

If traditional buy-and-holders ignore errant market valuations, then hedge funds (a metaphor for aggressive, "smart" capital) will force a reconciliation of true value to traded value. At times, the hedge funds can play a big part in creating bubbles, dislocations, and volatility, but more often than not they are part of a cure. Whether it was the global liquidity crisis resulting from LTCM's collapse in late 1998 or Bear Stearns's uncanny reprise of LTCM's uberleverage and subsequent illiquidity ten years later in 2008; or Société Générale's $7 billion in losses from Jérôme Kerviel's unauthorized trades, the markets blinked, for sure. But just a few years before, such ripples would have caused worldwide trauma without the rapid and aggressive reaction of alternative investors. Darwin prevails: some die; others thrive. Even now, as I write, vulture funds are snapping up the many broken pieces after the mortgage meltdown of 2007 and 2008.

You might ask, "Well, where are all these profits being made? Someone has to lose, right? It's not magic!" Yes, it is true. And who is the loser? Academics might answer that question better than I can, but I believe it is probably the traditional long-only investor: Mutual funds. Pension funds. Main Street. The hidden cost of active trading is greater market volatility, which is the waste product of leveraged speculation. Historically, traditional long-only investors—like pension funds and mutual funds—were able to buy securities only, so that market prices did not always reflect fair value. Prices were upward trending and sticky, so valuations did not always reflect the underlying opportunity or dysfunction. A long-only investor in XYZ security at, say, $10 per share would profit if the stock went from $10 to $8, then back to $12. The investor would know a 20 percent return. The hedge fund manager under the same market conditions may, seeing an opportune trend, drive the stock through short pressure down to $7 per share, cover the short, and buy it again at $8 per share, then ride it to $12 for a total profit of 80 percent—even more if he used leverage or options. Did the long-only investor lose money? No. But he saw higher volatility, and the hedge fund bandit benefited from it.

Diamonds in the Trash

Aside from pure market volatility, aggressive capital can change corporate policy through market action. Consider the fictional company of Barry Bling-A-Lot Jewelers. Barry the CEO does a great business selling diamonds. The demand for diamonds is high, and buyers are willing to pay big bucks to have them. Barry's business is profitable, but he is not a fastidious manager. Barry's laid-back style results in the company inadvertently and unknowingly throwing away a hundred diamonds nightly in the garbage.

Nevertheless, everyone appears content. Barry is making money. He could make more if he were not losing a hundred diamonds a night in the trash, but he is content. Customers are happy because they have plenty of bling to buy.

Then, searching Barry's trash, a forager stumbles on the hidden treasures, as, say, did Chanos with Enron. The discarded diamonds are a windfall. The forager knows that the scope of his fortune is directly proportional to his keeping the find to himself. He keeps quiet and continues to benefit. Soon, however, his fellow foragers cannot help but notice that the first forager looks healthier and wears better clothes. Other curious foragers catch on and follow suit. The wealth distribution to more and more foragers continues, but there is still enough to go around.

Eventually the number of foragers increases at the waste bins until the finds are not what they once were. As the crowd grows, only a lucky few are able to capitalize on the treasure offered by the diamonds. The more enterprising begin to forage elsewhere.

Traditional customers ultimately discover that foragers get the same high-quality goods for a lot less. Barry is compelled by his traditional customers to become more efficient. Diamonds no longer land in the garbage. In the process, Barry makes more per unit of diamond, and eventually diamond prices fall for the traditional customer.

So it is with hedge funds. This far-fetched analogy serves a purpose: the diamonds represent market value and the foragers are hungry hedge funds seeking hidden value, the "diamonds in the rough." Barry's customers represent the long-only traditional pension funds and other traditional investors. Barry collectively represents the publicly traded companies that comprise the market. The crowds, the latecomers, represent the move to higher productivity (no more wasted diamonds) that ultimately comes as a result of the foragers. Eventually, the spigot of lost opportunity value is turned off due to market pressure; in the process, the system becomes better, and the inefficiencies are closed. The final result is an improvement in Barry's operation, which redounds to the traditional customers. Everyone ultimately benefits.

A real-life example of the active market forcing a recalibration of value is the JPMorgan tactical acquisition of Bear Stearns. In March 2008, with the assistance of the Fed, JPMorgan agreed in an emergency transaction to acquire Bear Stearns for $2 per share, down from $30 the previous trading day. The fire-sale price was due to a run on the bank of Bear, causing a massive margin call on the bank and its eventual failure. Many people read the newspaper reports and just thought "Damn, that sucks." Others, like myself, thought, "Hey, that $2 seems a little off" and made trades reflecting that sentiment. In the following three business days, shares of Bear traded up from

$2 per share to $7 per share, *forcing* JPMorgan to up its bid to $10 per share in order for the transaction to have any hope of success. The traders buying the shares definitely risked losing: any trader who bought shares at greater than $2 would have lost all of the difference if the Morgan deal had closed as originally negotiated. Instead, armed with a little insight, a little number-crunching and, yes, a little luck, hedge funds *created* value fivefold, forcing a transaction of $1 billion plus instead of $250 million.[4] Intelligent capital creates value for itself and for the man on the street by reconciling true value and demanding operational and market efficiency.

Such is how a foraging market renders value.

No matter what assets are in your account—cash, stocks, bonds, futures, or commodities—they are constantly being assessed and reassessed by the market. What does that mean? A dynamic market consensus makes values "truer." In your own job—whatever it is—you would have no idea of your market value, your salary potential, until the market assessed and made offers for your labor. Without testing the market, i.e., sending out your résumé routinely,[5] for example, you might have no idea that a company may be interested in paying you more for the same services. You might get stuck making $25,000 with no upside, instead of twice as much with the possibility of upward mobility. In a similar way, the market liquidity provided by trading (often but not exclusively driven by hedge funds) tests and retests company value and ensures that through the process, the true market worth is determined.

---

4. The transaction is unresolved as of this writing.
5. I recommend that young job-seekers send out their résumés routinely even after they have found a job. One should constantly reassess and reevaluate one's own market value.

Hedge Funds, Activist Investing, and Regulation

Active investor involvement in company strategy and management is part of a growing area in alternative investing known as activist investing. "Activist investor" is today's term for the corporate raider of the 1980s. Icahn, for example, was a corporate raider in the 1980s; now he is considered an activist investor. He is doing the same thing; only the name has changed. And a lot more managers are looking for this type of opportunity. An activist investor finds companies that aren't doing as well as they should be. The activist investor accumulates ownership in a company until he owns a substantial share. Then he offers bellicose advice on ways to improve and kicks management in the posterior.

Before poor Barry discovers that he is throwing diamonds out the door, an activist manager might buy Barry's company. He would fire Barry (but keep his trade name, of course) and bring in the talent to run the ship with the precision it deserves rather than wait for Barry to clean up his act. Once the activist manager cures the inefficiencies, the activist manager can retain the benefits of higher diamond output for himself and more. Such ruthless pursuit of capital opportunity and profit was caricatured, obtusely, in the film *Wall Street*, in which Michael Douglas played a greedy, ruthless hedge fund bastard. "Greed is good," he quipped. I cannot disagree although I think as a corporate raider, ol' Gordon might have sported a better haircut and suit today.

There is a rising chorus of legislators calling for regulation of the investment activities of aggressive activist capital. In fact, Secretary of the Treasury Henry Paulson recently proposed sweeping changes to the regulation of the financial industry in the United States. The opponents of hedge funds and aggressive trading strategies point to the human cost of lost jobs, market turmoil, and ravaged pension plans. They have a point. But regulation is not the answer. The markets are compelled to self-adjust and thereby self-regulate.

Those supporting regulation suggest that the capital markets would continue to have such extreme cycles if left to their own ways. Policy makers worry that the foragers—hedge fund managers—would continue to pursue greed to their own peril and that of the planet. Such sentiment was evident in the tone with which the New York Fed announced that it was bailing out LTCM: "LTCM was so big that the Federal Reserve Bank of New York took the unprecedented step of facilitating a bailout of the private hedge fund, out of fear that a forced liquidation might ravage world markets."[6]

My view is that the markets will always correct themselves ultimately to the better result. Extreme market events, the tail events, the bad events that are supposed to happen every twenty years, can wreak havoc in the short term, but with an open market, there is an intrinsic self-correcting counterforce. When one door closes, another door opens. The surging market price of oil, for example, is a real problem right now. It inspires great fear as it climbs toward $200 a barrel, according to some estimates, and rightly so. I do not intend to sound cavalier. I recognize the great difficulty that the high price of oil poses to corporations and ordinary people trying to make ends meet. The answer, however, is not to render oil artificially cheap, as some have suggested. Yes, we could release the United States' strategic reserves or promote further drilling in even more difficult places or beg the Saudis, hat in hand, to pump out more. These interventions may work in the short term but would also encourage even more consumption of a dwindling resource.

The right answer is to let oil prices continue to rise. In-

---

6. Philippe Jorion.

dustries would, as a result, not be able to be profligate and profitable at the same time. The markets would force an adjustment. People would stop buying Hummers, and it would become prohibitively expensive to leave the incandescent lights on in the house. Maybe consumers would make greater use of renewable energy in their houses and cars, which is an inherently better long-term solution than continuing to burn fossil fuels unabated. Companies—and people—will adjust or perish. The solution will largely be rendered on the incentives and disincentives of the free market.

Thousands of cities across the United States have already begun to make adjustments to consume less energy, from using high-efficiency light-emitting diodes (LEDs) in traffic lights to planting gardens on rooftops, which can result in as much as a 25 percent reduction in energy consumption from climate control. "People forget, wind and solar power are here, they work, they can go on your roof tomorrow," reports Thomas Friedman in the *New York Times* ("Mr. Bush, Lead or Leave," June 22, 2008). "What they need now is a big U.S. market where lots of manufacturers have an incentive to install solar panels and wind turbines—because the more they do, the more these technologies would move down the learning curve, become cheaper, and be able to compete directly with coal, oil, and nuclear, without subsidies."

In the summer of 2007, I rented a Prius to drive down the coast of Croatia. It did occur to me to rent something fancier, but with the double dose of high gasoline prices and a weak dollar, I was compelled to moderation. The "green" car option was not even available until recently, even though the technology has long existed, until the market forced it. These adaptations occurred because buyers and sellers, the markets, compelled change. And change occurred. Toyota has increased production of the Prius by 60 percent for 2008.

Further evidence of the market giving impetus to industry adjustment may be found in metals recycling. There is a market afoot to "mine gold and other precious metals from mobile phones. [A] tonne of ore from a rather average gold mine produces on the order of five grams of gold. Some mines yield more; some less, but this is a good working average. Thus it is interesting to note that a tonne of scrapped mobile phones can yield 150 grams of gold or more according to a study done by Yokohama Metal. Further, this same [tonne] of discarded mobile phones also contains 100 kilograms of copper and three kilograms of silver. Is there any wonder why recycling has become so important in recent years? It is not because of ecological concerns; it is because economics trumps all else. The market works!"[7]

It is true that regulation can smooth out the potential extremes of purely market-driven policy, but open markets have shown a great deal of resiliency. "There is always a bull market somewhere," the saying goes. When hidden value can be foraged by hedge fund activity, it is usually because somehow economic services and assets can be done better or priced better. Smart money with velocity and size will ensure that that happens.

The capital markets will never be totally efficient. After all, markets are comprised of ordinary, whimsical people (and their computers) and are therefore subject to human emotions and frailties. But nimble capital is prone to sniff out discrepancies in the balance of risk, reward, and market prices, and thereby move the market toward greater efficiency. Where Icahn has increased company value by shining his attention on it, it makes him wealthy, but it does pretty well for other market participants, too, directly and indirectly. Hedge funds matter because low(er) productivity is a waste, just as it is a

7. Dennis Gartman, "The Gartman Letter," April 28, 2008.

waste for you to be paid less than you are worth in your job. Hedge funds buy and short-sell value in order to achieve better valuations and force assets and companies to higher efficiency. The proof of the trend toward efficiency pricing is that it is way harder to extract excess return from the markets now than it was ten years ago. The reason is that the easy ops—the diamonds in the waste bin—are harder to come by. That's a great thing. Barry Bling-A-Lot has cleaned up his act.

CHAPTER 4

KEY MARKET FACTORS: INVESTING IN THEMES

In the 1990s, day-trading was huge. Trading costs were low, the cable channels provided "trader talk" to fuel investment ideas, and discount brokers actively courted business from small investors. The barriers to entry were relatively low for new traders. I called it the trader's trap. The small investor was promised riches beyond belief simply by showing up and left-clicking his mouse. This phenomenon did not last long, however. As new investors watched their retail accounts dwindle over time, it became clear that successful profit-making was more difficult than the financial news anchors would have us believe. There is scarcely anyone bouncing about the great benefits of day-trading today. That is because yesterday's day trader is today's speculative real estate investor. And the frenetic buying and selling of real estate has had much the same impact. Today's subprime mess is yesterday's tech bubble.

There are infinite ways to turn a profit. Investing in longer-term macro trends will nonetheless generate more consistent profits. There is always a trend in *some* asset or sector that makes a compelling long-term trade. In my experience it is prudent to stay away from hyperactive day-trading to make money. There are hedge funds that still do it, but their profit margins have significantly diminished. Hyperactive trading has run its course because the gravy has been arbed out, but it leaves behind an opportunity. Today, the information gap for the small and large investor has narrowed a great deal. Profitable trading is directly dependent on superior information and judgment as opposed to blind stabs and good luck.

You would also be well advised to avoid the market televangelists. I am amused when, in the same week, the financial tabloids and the tele-journalists attribute a market rally on Monday to market optimism and then lament a sharp decline two days later on Wednesday and attribute it to market pessimism. The world just doesn't change that much in forty-eight hours. Stock valuations fluctuate but trying to trade the noise is a recipe for losing money.

Years ago, I had just left a hedge fund as a portfolio manager—rather unceremoniously, I must confess. I had been developing a quantitative trading model for some years and had finally received a mandate to run more than $100 million. As the debut for the model it was quite a nice number. I performed well: I was an "island," me and my computer, without any needs or interaction with the rest of my colleagues at the hedge fund. And all was fine until the CEO gave me an ultimatum: show me how it works, let me look up your kimono, or leave the firm. Given the years of development that had gone into it, I chose the latter. I packed my desk and was escorted out of the building by security in a dramatic Wall Street "perp walk." It was reminiscent of the scene from *The Odd Couple*, when Felix is shown the door clutching his frying pan.

I decided that I did not want to join another hedge fund group—the jockeying for capital to invest and for credibility at hedge funds can be quite fierce, and I was tired of that. Hedge funds are called firms but really they are something less structured. They are very linear institutions stuffed with bright people with one intention: to make money. For the trader inside the hedge fund, there really is no need to know or to talk to anyone else. There is no company slogan or mascot, and there is no cheerful banter at the water cooler. There is little incentive for idle chitchat. Maybe a trader looks tired or nervous—that would give away the current status of his p&l[1]. It could signal that the trader's "book"—that portion of the hedge fund's money he is investing in the market—is not doing so well. A side comment about the market might give another trader a great idea. Why give away information that could be used against you or could be used in the market by someone else who would profit instead of you? So I figured that I had had enough of that dynamic. I scraped together some capital to trade on my own and sought the services of a hedge fund hotel.

Hedge fund hotels are offices set up by brokerage firms, sometimes schlocky firms, so that young hedge funds or independent traders can get up and running immediately. The hotels provide the infrastructure necessary to run a hedge fund from day one. The traders do not have to worry about setting up the Internet, waiting for phone installations, hiring support personnel, negotiating trade-execution contracts, etc. The hotel "management" has everything ready.

My intention was not to day-trade but to do what you, the reader, are probably looking to do now: make money by trading my own book (portfolio) in a way that would be impervious to market swings. I wanted to identify longer-term themes, avoid volatility, and make consistent profits. I also hoped that if I didn't show up for a day or two or if I chose not to look at my p&l for a day or so, it would not make one bit of

---

1. Profit and loss statement.

difference in the performance of my portfolio. I found a firm that would give me a seat at a trading desk and provided clearing arrangements so that I could trade on their floor among other like-minded but independent traders.

In structure, it resembled a day-trading operation in that I had an account with my own money, but I used everything of theirs to administer it, including screens, data, telephone, desk, office, etc. The clearing arrangements were not so different from those in a regular brokerage account except that I was offered 4 to 1 leverage and trade execution at a penny per share. The 4 to 1 leverage was the OPM available to me to superweight my trades, if I decided to make use of it.

Having come from a pedigree firm, I was, at first, stunned on my arrival at the new environs. Most financial buildings have deep security in the lobbies. One's arrival in the typical New York lobby of a hedge fund is like a full-on interview process. "Who are you here to see?" "What company are you from?" "Can I see a picture ID?" "Speak into this microphone and say your name." "What was your income last year?" But this new building had none. No picture-taking, no reception, no retinal scans, no key cards, nothing. Not this place. This place was a Class B building. Its glory days were probably right before the stock market crash of 1929 and the onset of the Great Depression, from which it appeared it had never recovered. The door to the entrance was open to the street. The elevator wheezed down to the first floor.

It was a Friday. I learned later that Friday was the free-lunch day. Boxes of pizzas sat in a small kitchen to my left as I walked toward the receptionist. Her lips were newly painted, bright red and wet. Her cleavage was long and deeply cleaved. She was chewing gum and greeted me as if we had not seen each other in years. We had not; I did not know her. She alerted the administrator of the hotel by telephone that I was in the reception area.

Then she reached her head around the corner and yelled, "Goys, the pizza is hee-ya!" with a strong Staten Island accent. In a short while, the kitchen was full of traders. The traders slower to react to the cattle call formed a line down the hall for their turn in the kitchen and the free pizza. I thought about how strange it was that people would profess loyalty for life if you just give 'em a free lunch. Many hedge funds offer free lunch to the traders, though. It keeps them at or near their desks, undisturbed, while the market is open. "Let them eat cake!"

I was mortified by the sight of my fellow traders. What a motley collection of amateur investors they were! They had the dream of making millions by their wits, but they had neither the substance nor the discipline to accomplish it. Some of them looked as if they hadn't left their desks in days; they looked like those crazed souls you see compulsively feeding money into slot machines in the casinos. Many of the traders were superstitious of light (and hygiene, for that matter). The curtains were drawn, and the lights were out. "Traders hate the daylight," the receptionist chimed knowingly.

The room was dank and smelled like feet. A drab gray permeated all the furniture and carpeting, and most of it was very worn. As the administrator walked me back to my station, I spied the reactions of the hotel's market savants to the movements of their positions from moment to moment. They emitted gleeful squeals when the markets advanced or exasperated grunts when they declined. It was as if they were playing video games. My place amongst the rows of would-be Soroses was in a dusty laminate cubicle with an aged computer and a Herman Miller Aeron chair that was missing an arm. The other Soroses looked at me askance because I alone—probably in the entire building—was wearing a suit and tie. Everyone else was in jeans and sweat suits.

"Yo! Dude, *Dude*!" one exclaimed excitedly in a strong

New York accent as I was getting settled. He pointed excitedly at the screen, bouncing in his chair, seeking the attention of anyone in the vicinity. The other Soroses barely looked up, completely disinterested. I got the impression that they had heard the pleas of imminent opportunities from this genius plenty of times before. Those "opportunities" obviously must have been rarely profitable. "Dude—yo! It's goin' up. *Buy it*, dude. Buy it *now*!" I thanked him for the tip, but I was a little rattled. This place was supposed to be one of the premiere shops for housing independent hedge fund traders. "Is this how these independent traders make money?" I wondered. They all seemed hopeful to plead their positions in the right (profitable) direction, like little boys cheering on toy sailboats in a slow wind. Suddenly the prick who gave me the ultimatum at the old hedge fund did not seem like such a bad guy after all. "I wonder if I still have his number. Is he in the office today?" I thought to myself.

It didn't take me long to realize that this approach to the markets was not for me. I was, after all, a solid trader with experience at Morgan Stanley, First Boston, and a few hedge funds. I had been running $100 million! These guys looked like they wouldn't eat well if their sailboats didn't blow the right way. What freaked me out was that here was all this supposedly professional activity in what was supposed to be a professional setting with people who were supposed to know what they were doing, and yet most of them, I quickly learned, had absolutely *no* discipline. They had no techniques, no overriding principles, no apparent entrance or exit strategy, no system, and really, they had no portfolios. They performed only the frenetic action of a hardened gambler. They had no sense of how to discern, develop, execute, and reap profit from a great investment idea. But they were doing what I guess is the popular conception of what hedge fund trading is.

Indeed, going to the second tier from the top rank of traders is a far fall indeed. I never went back. Not even once. I
rented my own offices on an abandoned trading floor in a
nicer building near Wall Street. It was not as glamorous as
it may sound. I rented it from a failed brokerage from the
1980s that basically held the floor for document storage as
far as I could tell. Even scarier, they seemed to appreciate
the new income source from me, and—trust me—I was not
paying much. But it was really cool that I had an entire floor
of a building to myself. It was not long before I started a little
business subletting out the space to other companies. In addition to trading, I set up a minihotel myself, which turned
out to be not such a bad side business.

Anyway, the main lesson I am trying to drive home is that
discipline, information, and a discerning eye are the most
important requirements for successful trading. This applies
true to you, too, as you develop your own hedge strategy.
Sustainable, profitable hedge strategies are based on trading major themes in the market. Trading themes is far more
effective than the crazed buying and selling that was epito-
mized by my brief adventure in the world of day-trading,
circa 2003.

How to Find a Theme

Modern portfolio theory (MPT) is predicated on the idea
that there are five primary indicators,[2] market *factors*, that
move the markets and affect individual security prices, including stocks, bonds, and commodities. The fundamentals of
identifying market factors are the overwhelming reason that
great traders prevail. These market factors will be the foundation for the development of your own hedge strategy. The five

---

2. Stephen Ross and Richard Roll.

primary market movers are listed below. I like to call them the Fave Five:

1. The growth or decay of the Gross National Product and the business cycle
2. Expectations on the direction of interest rates
3. Consumer Confidence: two-thirds of the economy is based on the consumer
4. Short-term inflation
5. Long-term inflationary expectation (for example, anticipated increases in energy, food, or oil prices)

As noted, a successful hedge fund approach will not necessarily depend on highly active trading. In fact, for the average investor, trying to invest on a tick-by-tick, minute-by-minute basis is a surefire way to lose money. Having said that, even successful (profitable) traders will show that they are "right" only about 50 percent of the time *or less*. Discipline ensures, however, that the wins stay on longer, and the losses are cut short. Do not expect to be right all the time. No one is. Professional traders have advantages over the average trader as a result of the boundless, instantaneous market data they get, as well as trading floor "color"—the chatter that pervades the Street when a market event is imminent. It is not the percentage of times a trader is right on a trade that separates the great trader from the poor trader; it is his system for reaping profits and controlling losses. And frenetic trading does neither.

That is not to say that active trading strategies never profit because of course, when expertly executed, they do. But for the average investor, these sources of profits are not the low-hanging fruit. If you feel the urge to look at your book hourly or even daily, you probably need to reassess your strategy. The best way to effect a great hedge strategy is to invest in longer-term themes that, when combined, collectively ensure that you will achieve profits irrespective of what the market is doing.

The challenge is to determine what effect the five major market factors will have on individual stocks or other financial securities in which you may invest. Every security will have some sensitivity to each market factor, but determining which market factors will have the greatest impact on the price of a particular security is the trick.

Sometimes finding an actionable corelationship between market factors and security prices is easy. We know, for example, that utility stocks are usually high-dividending stocks analogous to fixed-income securities. Therefore, utility stocks are particularly sensitive to changes in interest rates. We also know that the common stock securities of consumer-product companies do well when Consumer Confidence is high. But things change. Every day, new information becomes available as economic conditions or expectations change, and these will have a direct impact on your portfolio choices.

The Fave Five are very high-level indicators, but they work as a starting point for finding your way. It is important to keep these general relationships in mind. Here is a basic example. Around October 2007, the Fed was forced to start lowering interest rates (Fave Five #2) as a result of the liquidity concerns stemming from the rising tide of mortgage defaults and their impact on financial institutions and the global credit markets. But the Fed was between a rock and another rock. Leave rates alone and risk virtual meltdown of global liquidity and credit, or lower rates aggressively, potentially creating an overheated economy and therefore causing inflation (check Fave Five #5). Inflation can be real poison to economic growth because costs increase, but not necessarily revenues. The higher cost of fuel and the shrinking dollar also contributed to inflationary pressures. I first noticed this when my three small grocery bags added up to $125. What do you think happens when things get more expensive? People make fewer discretionary expenditures like, iPods, cool clothes, and cell phones. One would expect the stocks of companies that sell discretionary items to suffer—and that is exactly what happened.

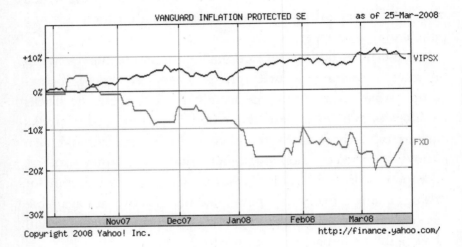

Above we have a graph of the Vanguard Inflation Protected Securities Fund (VIPSX) versus an index of consumer discretionary companies, First Trust Consumer Discretionary AlphaDEX Fund (FXD). The VIPSX benefits from inflation, and FXD is an index of the health of companies selling and manufacturing discretionary consumer products. You get the picture: the expectation of inflation cooled the jets on discretionary expenditures, and therefore the stocks of those companies declined.

Now, let us look at Fave Five #1 during the same time period. Instead of considering Gross National Product, let us consider Gross Sector Product, which is revenue for a sector of the economy instead of the economy of the whole country. Above we noted that liquidity was tight. What does that *mean*? Well, banks provide liquidity: they borrow at one rate, then lend most of it out at a higher rate to make profits. If liquidity is tightening, that would mean that banks probably are not lending as much. As a consequence, banks were making less money. And that is exactly what happened. Below, for the same period, is the index ETF for the U.S. financial sector (XLF) overlaid on the same graph:

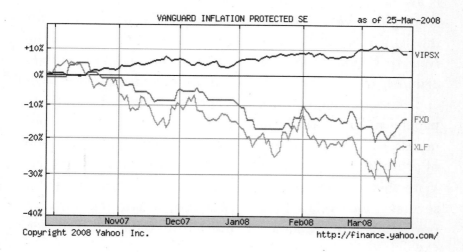

I know what you are thinking. "That's too easy and in hindsight." Not true. I swear that every trader and his mother moved on these trades in 2007. They were long inflationary hedges, like gold, and short financials and consumer cyclicals. And most made money with that trade. Really, the only thing that distinguished the good traders from the ones who didn't do well is whether they came late to the party or were the last ones to leave. As soon as the Fed started to cut rates, this phenomenon began to express itself. Note the length of the trade, too. The guys who day-traded this trend probably did not do well. Only the ones who stuck with the theme over the course of the year earned the breadth of the move.

You might complain again, "Where the hell will I get data for this stuff? How would I know these movements were going on? Data is expensive!" Hardly. First, I intentionally used graphs from Yahoo! Finance because it is a free online service, and it puts tons of financial information at your fingertips. Moreover, high-level trend information is available in the daily newspaper. That's right, I am suggesting that you read. Believe it: a great starting point for investing ideas is the daily national newspapers, such as the *New York Times*, the *Washington Post*, *International Herald Tribune*, and, of course, the *Wall Street Journal*. All market and economic happenings are reported responsibly in these papers and in their headlines. These publications do not necessarily offer trading advice, but they *will* inform you of prevailing trends that you can exploit to your advantage. With this data and a little imagination you can put together several theme-related trades and hedge them in your own portfolio. Here are some headlines from today's newspaper. (March 2008):

- "Oracle's Profit Rises, but Shares Fall" [What does that portend for the industry?]
- "Motorola Moves to Split Itself into Two" [Seems the telecom industry may be suffering, even more.]
- "Dow Falls After 2 Downbeat Reports: A pair of pessimistic reports on home sales and business spending reminded investors about the precarious state of the economy." [Duh!]

Information contained in these publications can be used to shape your broad investment themes: a major company announcing a new development campaign; significant layoffs in a particular industry; effects of disruptive technologies, such as, say, the effects of digital photography on print photo manufacturers (Eastman Kodak was a volatile but profitable short sell for many months in the early 2000s); earnings announcements; global macroeconomic trends; news about China and other emerging markets; the status of the American dollar; trade deficits/surpluses; and geopolitical incidents and developments. These kinds of stories all have consequences in the investment markets, and they are all reported on a daily basis in the national and international newspapers.

The second most important aspect of devising a macro trading strategy for the do-it-yourselfers is keeping your eyes open for opportunities and being creative in expressing your investment ideas with available financial instruments. This is where true value is realized. Clearly, information is most valuable when it can be used to turn a profit. Remember to use good news and bad news, too. Keep an open mind about how to capitalize on bad news or a poor outlook for a company, for an industry, or for an economy (globally) as much as you would positive news. In most instances, this is where the hedge trade is made by being on both sides of an opportunity.

I have mentioned that Eastman Kodak was a volatile long-term short. Did you immediately think to yourself, "Yeah, but how would I hedge out my exposure by controlling risk?" Did it occur to you that a single unhedged trade bears the full brunt of market risk? You did, and I am proud of you. As it turns out FUJIFILM was an excellent hedge against a short of Eastman Kodak because of FUJIFILM's diversified product offering. Since 2000, this long-term hedge paid quite well, 50 percent, with limited volatility as a result of the hedge.

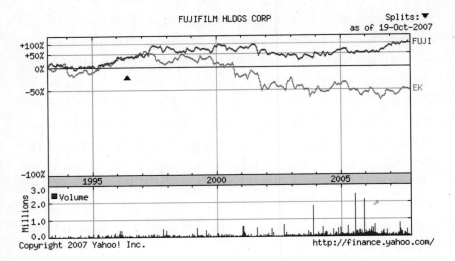

Investing in themes and hedges requires a particular mind-set. It takes some training and practice, but, truly, you can turn everyday news into trading profits.

One of my great friends, Moishe Lowenstein, runs a successful hedge fund, and his success is even more striking because he has no capital in his hedge fund. How is this possible, you may ask? Well, he raises money from other people to invest in his trade ideas on an as-needed basis. He raises money for investing in themes, so these trade ideas need to be really good for people to dig into their pockets on demand. Technically, he runs a hedge fund, but there is actually little hedging.

I learned an early lesson on being "market-alert" from Moishe while we were engaged in one of our favorite summer pastimes. Every summer, we would rent a charming old house to share in Bridgehampton, New York. Although the Hamptons are only about ninety miles from New York City, it can be quite a schlep to make the trip every weekend, especially if you have to lug things back and forth. Moishe therefore liked to store his "toys" in the Hamptons during the winter instead of storing them in Manhattan just to schlep them back out just a few months later. Such effects included his boat, the summer furniture (which could not be left in the house through the winter), and the pink pants emblazoned with green elephants that he was fond of wearing.

One summer, Moishe needed to store more than the usual items after a summer of spirited shopping facilitated by a great year with his investments. He needed to rent a larger storage space. He noted aloud as we were packing up the house that the storage facilities in the Hamptons were a great deal, because they charged approximately 30 percent less than did storage facilities in Manhattan.

Strange, he thought to himself. It doesn't make sense. Most renters of storage space in the Hamptons are New Yorkers. If they rent storage space in the city, they are accustomed to paying substantially more. Moreover, the people who rent and own houses in the Hamptons are generally financially well off, inasmuch as summer rentals can cost $30,000 to $50,000 per month.

So how is it, he wondered, that the wealthiest New Yorkers pay huge rental rates to enjoy homes in the Hamptons, while at the same time they were getting bargain rates for their storage spaces? Demand was high as well, with occupancy rates for storage spaces higher than 80 percent.

Moishe realized that there was the potential for the kind of layup arbitrage on LES lemonade that we discussed in chapter 2. You have the same pool of buyers, separated by a small geographic span, buying the same good at vastly different prices while demand is high. Moishe concluded that if he bought all the storage providers in the Hamptons, he would be able to immediately raise prices and take a profit. Then he could repackage and sell the same facilities at a higher price. Though unconventional, this was a classic trend-following trade.

But Moishe had to be sure that this opportunity was actually as good as it seemed. Lots of details had to be analyzed, such as the risk that raising prices might drive renters elsewhere or spur others to build similar facilities. Moishe knew, however, that the towns in the Hamptons were relatively development-averse, and there were only three storage facilities servicing the entire area. In other words, if he could buy all three facilities, there would be nothing to stop him from raising prices.

In short, Moishe purchased all three facilities. He solicited investors into his directional, trend-following hedge fund set up specifically to make this trade. These special vehicles are called, strangely, special-purpose acquisition companies (SPACs). He brought in approximately twenty investors to raise $11 million. Each investor was bound to confidentiality so that they could not steal Moishe's idea. He purchased the properties for $11 million, raised prices (and services), and later sold them for $21 million, taking a handsome profit. Oh, and he didn't put up any money of his own but took a good share of the profits.

This is not a trade on the stock market, but I use the story frequently to illustrate the need to look for the hidden value. Before making a trade, always ask yourself "What are other people *missing*?" As far as the Hamptons storage goes, anyone could have made the same trade Moishe did, but no one else saw it. Hell, I wish I had thought of it. I encourage the new trader to examine ordinary news on a daily basis and think specifically, "How can I trade this information? How can I use it to make money?"

I have another Moishe story, which illustrates the seemingly obvious benefit of taking business themes from the national newspapers. The "green" movement has caught the eye of investors, as it has become clear that alternative energy sources will be essential to sustain our way of life. One day, while reading the newspaper, Moishe noticed a short article in the *Wall Street Journal* which noted that an alternative energy company called ABC Battery had recently raised $2 million in funding. The article also mentioned that ABC had scarce revenue but had closed a deal to sell its products to the State of California, a pioneer in the use of alternative energy. ABC is an industrial battery company that makes zinc bromide batteries. Moishe was impressed with these two accomplishments made by such a small company, and he firmly believed the green trend would be sustained.

ABC's principal product was the design and manufacture of zinc bromide batteries. Zinc bromide batteries can provide energy at a substantial cost savings to industrial lead batteries, measured in cents per watt. Zinc bromide batteries are more durable than their counterparts; the ABC batteries, "Zincbats," can be drained further than lead batteries without causing damage. Once a lead battery is drawn to below 70 percent of total capacity, there is a risk that the battery could be irrevocably damaged. Zincbats are also capable of a sustained power drain, unlike lead acid batteries, which are capable of producing only short bursts of electrical current during, say, a brownout, but cannot sustain power generation for extended periods. Last, Zincbats can be drained multiple times, while lead acid batteries cannot.

One of the greatest attributes of the Zincbats is that the batteries can be charged from the electrical grid during the night, when demand and costs are low, then drained steadily for power during the day, lessening the cost of energy consumption. Also, based on his real estate experience, Moishe was aware that electricity costs during peak hours were significantly higher than energy costs during off hours.

Zincbats are also potentially useful in developing markets,

where electricity is not consistently available. News had been extensive about how residents of Iraq were forced to endure frequent power outages and brownouts. Moishe saw that this could be a growth market for ABC.

Moishe learned that the ABC Battery company had been successful in selling its batteries to industrial users who needed portable power such as at construction sites, but Moishe saw a turnkey opportunity by selling to California. Moishe called the company directly and asked to speak to the CEO. This was a bold move, but that is precisely what I want to convey: chutzpah and faith in your own analysis will uncover untouched possibilities and lead to original and profitable investment ideas. The talking heads on your financial news channels and at the investment banks simply warm up old information—call them leftovers—and peddle it to the less informed as opportunities and insights. *You* have the capacity to generate your own insights and initiatives.

It took a few calls, but after Moishe was able to interview the CEO, he confirmed that his ideas for the company were viable and actionable. In fact, after only a few weeks of negotiation, he locked up the rights to distribute the battery in Europe and the Middle East. He also purchased a substantial stake in the company, using the same formula he had for storage facilities in the Hamptons. He formed another SPAC and aggressively sought investors. Most of the people he approached invested, and he quickly raised $7 million. Two years later, the company had a secondary IPO, and Moishe made a substantial profit.

The point of this story, aside from the inspiration we can all take from Moishe's bold style, is that there are tradable treasures right there in your national newspaper. I know it sounds corny and obvious but just get in the habit of reading the headlines, the underlying stories, and ask yourself, "How can I profit from this?" Take the information you find in the news and turn it into long-term, exploitable action. Trolling for information that provides an edge is precisely what hedge fund managers do too. Of course, they also get really good chatter for the tick-to-tick opportunities, but theme identification and opportunistic investing is fundamental. Some ideas will work, and others will not. Abandon the ideas that don't work (over time), and ride the ones that do.

Here are a couple of things to note about my buddy Moishe:

1. Moishe got these ideas while reposing on a sofa, reading the Sunday newspaper, but had the mindset that tradable themes are a matter of *opportunity thinking.*

2. The size of these transactions may have you thinking, "I don't have that kind of money." Well, neither did Moishe—but he does, now. In neither of these deals did he invest his own capital, nor did he have the capacity to. Money follows great ideas.

I recognize that these examples are slightly different from your typical hedge fund trades, because they were semiprivate transactions and were directional in nature. But I like these stories because I refer to them myself when trying to stimulate myself to think. I think about the sheer, clever insightfulness of the Hamptons trade and the temerity of the ABC trade. I strive every day to find such gems, and these stories remind me that it can be done.

Use What You've Got

A great trade does not have to be glamorous. For the last twelve months, the business newspapers have often referred to the fall of the dollar versus other currencies. This may not stimulate a lot of action for the person not looking for it, but it screamed for an action from the circumspect trader. The decline in the dollar was partially the result of the Fed's low interest rates. When the currencies of other developed countries, of Europe, for example, yielded higher interest rates than the United States, it was a cinch to make a profitable risk-controlled carry trade.

A carry trade is selling one currency short and buying another currency that pays higher interest. For the 1990s the carry trade on every trader's book was the dollar/yen. Interest rates in Japan had been at or near zero for some time. Traders borrowed yen at no cost and invested in dollars or European currencies in great amounts and using great leverage. The trader executing a carry trade can trade billions while paying low or no interest on the euro-currencies or the dollar as the reward.

Anyway, back to the cratering U.S. dollar. This is a trade you could have found right there on the front page of the *Wall Street Journal*. It caught my attention, too. Like anybody else, I had to find a way to effect a trade in my personal accounts that took advantage of the dollar's sliding value. I took the money I had sitting in my savings account, let's say it was $100,000. In U.S. dollars, my account was yielding approximately 3.8 percent. But the dollar was increasingly weak relative to other international currencies, which, I believed, represented a better value. I called my bank and asked if I could convert my dollars to euros. "Yes, of course, Mr. Weddington," my banker said. My bank, like many banks today, has international branches and offers international currencies. So I simply transferred dollars from my savings account to an interest-bearing savings account in euros, paying 4 percent.

At first glance, it would seem that this would not be a very profitable trade. I took $100,000 out of my dollar savings account paying 3.8 percent and converted it to a euro account yielding 4.0 percent. The difference was only an additional 0.2 percent annually, or a paltry $200 annual difference. Big deal.

But since the dollar was weakening against the euro, the value of my money was increasing because of the exchange rate. With each cent that the dollar weakened, the return on the euro-currency I bought increased. So instead of earning only $200 per year, after two years, based on the interest rate differential, I earned more than 20 percent as represented by the change in value of the dollar versus the euro.

When I converted my euros back to dollars, I had $127,000. In other words, I "bought" euros by converting my U.S. dollars at an exchange rate of 1 euro to $1.10. I sold euros for dollars when the exchange rate was 1 euro to $1.37.

Just about any average Joe the Plumber who watches the news knew about this trend, though I believe few sought to take advantage of it. On the contrary, just about every diversified hedge fund in the world profited on it. Why not you? You did not need to have an account in Switzerland or even a brokerage account. In fact, the same trade could have been had by taking hard, physical cash—green dollar bills—and exchanging them at your local bank for the currency of your choice. That wouldn't be a particularly sophisticated method, but it is accessible and would have achieved the same result and the same return. Hustle!

Global Themes

We have established that great ideas come from traditional media and are readily available to you. All it takes to act on them is a little bit of imagination and gumption. Yet how many people called the CEO of ABC after the article that Moishe read appeared in the newspaper?

The currency trade could also have been your trade. It didn't require a lot of money to do it, and the media had been blaring about the opportunity. Moreover, in this case, the size of your investment didn't matter. Even a small investor could have executed the same trade. At 27 percent, an investment of $5,000 over the same two-year period would have returned $6,350. That's real money.

At the time of this writing, another theme is readily and glaringly apparent—the emergence of the economies of China and India. Investing in emerging markets can be a wild ride, and these two are no exception. So many of the opportunities are speculative and relatively illiquid at this stage of their economic development. But at least some capital should be allocated to the high-risk, high-reward trade. Okay, we have read our newspapers and are sufficiently curious. How can we get exposure?

The most direct way to get exposure to China and India is to invest directly, by way of purchasing public securities in Chinese or Indian companies on their local exchanges. That would be pretty advanced for the average investor. Frankly, it is hard enough to find good individual stock picks in the U.S. markets, with which you are already relatively familiar, let alone trying to understand foreign companies functioning in foreign markets. The accounting practices are different, the definition of income and cash flow are different, the currency is different. It is difficult territory to make direct investments in foreign markets if you do not have experience. Alternatively, one could invest directly in these emerging markets with American Depository Receipts (ADRs). ADRs are a little more approachable but harbor many of the same challenges as would investing directly.

It is not necessary to do so. There are plenty of Asian-market experts at your disposal. There is no shame in hiring other experts in your homegrown hedge fund. The big funds do it all the time: they hire other managers to add investment value. It is a common practice, and you can do the same.

In chapter 1, we spoke of specialized and sector-based hedge funds and ETFs. I like specialized mutual funds and particularly ETFs because you can get a professional manager managing your exposure to India or China. It's still your global idea; the ETFs simply provide assistance in implementing it. Prominent funds of this type are PowerShares Golden Dragon Halter USX China (PGJ), SPDR S&P China (GXC), UltraShort FTSE/Xinhua China 25 ProShares (FXP), and iShares FTSE/Xinhua China 25 Index (FXI). India ETFs include WisdomTree India Earnings Fund (EPI) and Power-Shares India Portfolio (PIN).

There is another way to get global exposure by simply purchasing U.S.-based companies. I only buy companies that are based in the United States,[3] but I have not wanted to miss the opportunity of investing in the emerging markets. I sought access to the emerging markets by trading U.S. companies that have significant business in Asia. Buying the stocks of U.S. companies operating in China and India is like buying my own portfolio-management team to manage my assets in emerging markets. There are many large companies that, although they are U.S.-based, invest heavily in the emerging markets of India and China. Such industries include technology, consumer products (say, Coca-Cola and Procter & Gamble), health care, and media. So my surrogate for getting exposure in the China and India markets is investing in companies that

---

3. When a hedge fund manager raises capital in a fund, he is specifically restricted to the strategy he has claimed he will run. That is known as the fund's mandate. So if I am a small-cap arbitrageur and small caps start losing money, I can't switch to the emerging markets or bonds because they are making money. That would be a no-no known as style drift.

have an intelligent emerging market strategy and significant presence there. It is tantamount to hiring some of the greatest minds in finance to run my international exposure. And the same strategy is available to you.

Below is a recent excerpt from "The Complete Investor," a financial newsletter edited by Stephen Leeb that, as a practice, seeks out U.S.-based companies that have a global reach.

Outside the natural resource sector, U.S. stocks with the strongest stake in the developing world will be the major beneficiaries of growth. However, when investing in the developing world, it is important to distinguish between companies domiciled in developing countries and American multinational companies expanding into those countries. . . .

U.S. companies such as Johnson & Johnson (JNJ), Coca Cola (KO), ITT Corp. (ITT), and others which have growing stakes in China will benefit in two important ways.

On the one hand, our [China and India] picks are taking advantage of the fastest growing consumer market in the world to grow their revenues. At the same time, they will profit from changing currency values. . . . Their remaining method is to allow their currencies to gain value. And that will mean greater profits for U.S. companies operating in [China and India].

Be Like Moishe

Whether it is buying ETFs, or U.S. companies with global exposure, or physically buying hard cash to effect a currency trade, there is always a way to express your investment view. Have the courage to ask yourself how.

For many Americans through the 1990s, the answer was day-trading, fulfilling the fantasy of participating with the big boys. It seemed sexy. Still today I grimace when I see TV commercials from brokerage firms, supposedly empowering the would-be investor to trade in his living room. It is a simple cheerleading—and it treats the would-be small investor as though he were playing in some kind of videogame. Do not fall into the false hope of trading like the caricatures in these commercials or in the movies. If you have to be sexy, be sexy like Warren Buffett.

Prices move for a reason, and understanding reasons behind securities' movement is essential to profitable trading. There is simply no escaping the wisdom of developing a comprehensive understanding of the forces that drive markets and price movements. You should be armed with the rationale and conviction to initiate a well-conceived trade. The Fave Five can provide you with such a framework.

Also, be like Moishe. I recounted Moishe's stories not because he is a hugely successful hedge fund trader but because he is a wide-eyed opportunist. Whenever I consider a new data point or opportunity, I ask myself, "What would Moishe do (besides perhaps change his name)?" "How can I make money here?" "Does it make sense?" "Is this my judgment or someone else's?" The more you know about the factors that move markets, the more things will make sense to you and the more tuned in you will be to finding great opportunities. Given the sheer number of traders and capital seeking the same thing—profits—your trading is a mere pimple, but why not be a pimple on the backside of a thoroughbred instead of a sow? Take the copious information that is readily available to you and have the courage to think!

CHAPTER 5

FINDING CORELATIONSHIPS

E vents in the capital markets follow themes. And they recur. Every trader eventually sees the changes on the horizon, some sooner than later. Really, we all know when changes are coming. Great traders are distinguished by how they prepare for what's on the horizon and how far in advance they can see. Warren Buffett famously apologized in 1999 for sticking to his guns and missing the advance of technology stocks. He had felt for some time that the stock market bubble was going to burst; he saw it coming on the horizon. He did not participate in the giddy excesses of the bull market in technology stocks. But the bubble lasted just long enough that he began to question his own wisdom. He acknowledged ruefully that perhaps he had missed an opportunity. But by autumn 2000, when the market had lost 39 percent in the NASDAQ, or $1.8 *trillion* in total market value, Buffet was vindicated, once again, as the Sage of Omaha.

Many profitable themes are slow moving, have extended onsets, and are well-covered by the media. They are not a secret, and they are there for all to participate in. Short-term opportunities are also available to the trader, but they are volatile in nature, short-lived, and usually based on short-term news, such as earnings surprises and disappointments.[1] "Firms that report a large positive earnings surprise do much better than expected in the future and firms that report a large negative earnings surprise do somewhat worse than expected."[2]

The objective for the investor is to "see" themes coming and position his portfolio to take advantage of their consequences. The trader should also hedge himself against the inevitable, contrary outcomes. You have to do both, because your chosen trades will not always be right. Some of your portfolio should be oriented toward the possibility that you could be wrong about your target themes. You should be positioned to take advantage of your insights, while hedged against unforeseen events.

Long-term themes can be obvious. For many traders, though, the obviousness is often seen in hindsight. The reason is that we get comfortable with the status quo because "the devil we know" uncertainty is easier to deal with than is the uncertainty of taking proactive steps. We know fundamental changes could be upon us, but to acknowledge it as a risk or opportunity compels an action. It is like anything else in life. It can be very difficult to be proactive—especially if you are making money through procrastination. For example, GM became a sloth because it was simply more personally advantageous for entrenched management to do nothing. Another example: Everyone knew the tech surge was near its end, but they were simply making too much money to change their course of action. Could a company

---

1. Most public companies tell investors ahead of time how much money they are going to make or lose. Once their books are closed and the money is counted, if the total is significantly different—plus or minus—than what they predicted, that is called an earnings surprise.
2. Russell Lundholm, Stephen M. Ross School of Business.

with no revenues really be worth $1 billion? Of course not! It was like musical chairs—we knew the music would stop, yet we continued to play the game undeterred. In one of the more comical turns, Mark Cuban shorted Yahoo! the moment they bought his company, Broadcast.com. Unlike so many at the time, Broadcast.com actually had revenue to the tune of $100 million. But the Yahoo! acquisition price of $5.9 billion reflected a whopping 59 to 1 price-to-revenue ratio. In only a few years after the Yahoo! acquisition, Broadcast.com was producing less than $20 million in revenue for Yahoo! There were other synergies provided to Yahoo!, of course, but at the end of the day, Cuban profited on his Yahoo! short position, didn't he?

The subprime crisis presented a similar investor dilemma. In short, the subprime crisis resulted in great liquidity strain as a result of a higher rate of defaults, overlending, and outright fraud. Mortgage brokers knew that they were providing mortgages, sometimes fraudulently, to people who could ill afford them. Adjustable-rate mortgage (ARM) borrowers certainly would not be able to afford the huge jumps in interest rate after the initial sweetheart period. Yet the brokers made millions in commissions, and Wall Street benefited from the flow of deals and therefore transaction fees. During the period in which Merrill Lynch participated in subprime investments, its stock was up almost 100 percent from $54 in May 2005 to $97 in January 2007.

By January 2007, there was already a loud drumbeat of concern over the easy money available in the mortgage market, yet Merrill stock continued to climb because investors (in Merrill) were seduced by the trend of profitability and ever-increasing deal flow. This was just what shareholders loved to see from Merrill's new CEO, Stanley O'Neal. The growing concern about mortgage exposure was simply an "inconvenient truth" that most investors preferred not to see and pretended did not exist. Yet it was more than visible—it was the elephant in the room!

By January 2008, Merrill stock was back down to $50, completing a full round trip and hurting a lot of people in the process—not just the bankers and the tasseled-loafer set but normal folk. It was evident to all that the trouble clouds were gathering on the horizon, yet we continued to invest in the stock until the only choice was to stampede out of it at lower prices. By September 2008, Merrill was out of business as a stand-alone company.

Recently, I paid a visit to Joseph, a friend who had been running a fund of funds (FOF). An FOF is a specialized hedge fund whose target investments are other hedge fund managers. Instead of picking stocks or other publicly traded investment instruments, the FOF picks other hedge funds in which to invest. FOFs were popular in the early days of hedge funds because there was very little information available on hedge fund performance at the time. The wealthy individual investor might have had trouble even *finding* a hedge fund in which to invest. FOFs would scour for the promising new managers of which the investor might be unaware. The second benefit of investing in a FOF is scale. The typical FOF minimum investment is generally lower than that of individual hedge funds. So an individual could more easily afford a FOF investment, plus get exposure to the performances of multiple hedge funds at the same time.

Joseph is a veteran in the business. He had been in the trenches, investing in some of the earliest "Market Wizards" from the very beginning. Frustrated with the performance of a few of his managers, Joseph decided to redeem all of the capital invested in hedge fund managers and run the investment strategies himself. "Why bother with the middle man?" he likely thought to himself. After all, he had spent a lot of time researching the right hedge managers in whom to invest. Such study, he thought, should be a skill transferable to the discipline of choosing stocks (companies) or investment themes.

I always liked Joseph. He was kind, erudite, and funny—a gentleman in a business of wolves. He was a natty dresser and always appeared perfectly coiffed, with his skin glowing as though he had just come fresh from the spa. He was also well connected and casually regaled me with personal stories about famous people whom most of us only read about.

Joseph had been an independent with his new solo enterprise for about a year when I called on him next. He had beautiful offices on Madison Avenue, right in the center of the triangle of majestic prewar office buildings. Walking onto his floor was like walking into a magnificent living room from *Town & Country*. Accordingly, he would always offer bialys, tea, or cappuccinos from the kitchen, his staff waiting only for his command. This time, though, he was different. The year he had spent managing his investors' capital directly had not been particularly agreeable. He was still cheery, but he was not the same man. In a word, he looked terrible. His hair was disheveled, his clothes were ill-fitting, and he had lost a lot of weight. He had gut-twisting halitosis.

We compared notes. I had had a pretty good year. Having switched from statistical arbitrage to a fundamental strategy, my numbers had been quite good. In 2007, I had returned over 42 percent net to my clients, which was at the top of all Long/Short US managers.[3] I mentioned some of my more profitable trades to Joseph: I was overweight in the sectors of Materials (gold), Energy, and (global) Industrials, and I was

---

3. HSBC/Altinvest manager universe.

selectively short individual names in Palm, the Telecom sector, and financials.[4]

"It wasn't a great year for me," he confessed. "I made many of the same trades you did, but when volatility kicked up, I sold my positions out of fear. Had I held on to them, I would have had the same performance you did."

I thought about that. He showed me examples of his trades, and it was true. All of the "brilliance" I had shown in the same year was obviously just as visible to my friend—and to anyone else who studies the markets. As much as I liked to think that I was a genius (I am not), my trading ideas were not unique. In fact, they were common. The only thing that separated us was that I suspect my friend was likely trading his positions almost daily instead of investing in the hedge. It reminded me of the frenetic freaks at the hedge fund hotel I had visited years prior, where if things went against them short term, they reacted with fear. They would forget all about the combination of themes that encouraged the investments in the first place. They had no sell discipline, no risk discipline, no size discipline, and no fundamental commitment to themes. If trouble arose, they would cut and run.

Reemphasis: Discipline

Once a theme has presented itself to you, you must have the patience to have it realize its potential or its lack of potential before you panic. This may sound contrary to the advice to take your losses early and move on, but it is not. Your conviction and reasoning in a trade based on a theme should be directly proportional to your staying power. The individual securities you choose to express your theme may require ad-

---

4. Severely oversimplified.

justment, or replacement, but your theme should nonetheless be given the time to breathe and evolve.

In January 2008, I got slaughtered (down 6 percent) by many of the same positions that rewarded me in the previous quarter. They got *hammered*, declining more than the market by a factor of two. But through my tears at the desk, I could still see the rationale of my positions. I did not sell or panic. The positions were the right ones, according to my logic and calculus. Hindsight would show that their disproportionate losses were caused by several hedge funds effectively liquidating (going out of business), so profitable positions were the ones they sold first in order to raise cash. Thus my own good positions suffered. My themes were back in the saddle by the end of the quarter.

There is no right discipline except the one that works for you. If you have clear targets for price performance and sound reasoning, your own investment rhythms will eventually emerge. If your trend or theme falters, do not impulsively run for cover. Reexamine your rationale. If it is a sound insight, then the opportunity will sustain itself. There are all sorts of reasons why a theme may show weakness or temporarily reverse. There are lots of market participants with their own agendas. Some traders test the strength of the market's conviction by selling against it. That creates volatility and shakes out the weak hands so that the experienced hand can make a profit or consolidate a position. The weak hands are the frenetic ones.

You do not have to trade out of a trend, stalled or not, if you think its fundamentals are sound. We discussed early on that it is entirely unlikely that you will think of a trade idea that has not already been conceived and put into play. The only real difference between you and any other investor is how you trade it. It all comes down to how long you stick to your guns and whether you are protected if you are wrong—in other words, hedged.

In the construction of your hedge portfolio, consider that there are many major market themes—the Fave Five and more—that are operating together like the voices in a choir. Like a choir, each market theme has a unique voice. At times, these multiple themes are dissonant and at other times they combine in such a way as to sound like the gospel. Hallelujah! Think of your hedge portfolio as the audience. While some of your portfolio may be tuned to the sopranos in the choir, other parts of your portfolio should be tuned to the tenors. At least some members of the audience, your portfolio, should be enjoying themselves. By having some component of your total portfolio tuned in to multiple independent market "voices," you stand a better chance at diversification—and, more important, you have provided a hedge against the full risk of the market's movements.

Diversification is the well-established key to the construction of a successful portfolio. But what I'm talking about here is more specific. Not only do you want to be diversified in your hedge portfolio, you want your portfolio to have elements that will benefit no matter what and to make sure those benefits will outperform your less-than-profitable positions. No trader can predict the future, but he can be prepared for multiple potential outcomes. Take exposure to the payouts you expect while also taking positions that will protect you if you are wrong.

After years of running statistical arbitrage (stat arb) strategies, computer-driven strategies based on just mathematical algorithms to select positions, I changed my investment approach because I was impressed by the consistent performance of the human stock pickers as compared to that of my purely computer-driven selection processes. Starting in the early 2000s, in a period when "known" relationships between investable assets began to be less predictable because of once-in-a-generation global events, stat arb lost its performance edge to the research analysts. Not to be outdone, I was convinced that I could do what they did by quantifying a fundamental thinking process. I needed to return to traditional analysis out of necessity. Stat arb was not returning what it once did. It turns out that all of those backward-thinking fundamental researchers I once disdained were pretty smart after all. You know, the ones who wax eloquent about price/earnings ratios, debt/equity ratios, EBITDA, and the like. I set about developing a rule-based fundamental selection process for investing in the markets.

I discovered a lot implementing my new approach. I started by identifying the sectors in which I wanted to buy or sell short, and then I identified the companies within those sectors that would achieve the sector's anticipated performance or better. I identified candidates by targeting growth companies within a sector at a discount to their peers. I executed short sales on the securities at the bottom of my criteria, or stocks that I anticipated would underperform relative to their peers. I maintained a core portion of the portfolio devoted to shorts.

By identifying the sectors to own based on approaching market conditions and actively selling sectors or individual securities I thought were weak or overvalued, I created a natural hedge in the portfolio. I was long sectors that would do well in 2007—consumer staples, health care, industrials. I also identified sectors that would do well if the market really went south—commodities (due to a weakening dollar), energy (due to increasing demand and the growing interest in alternative energies), currencies (against a weakening dollar), and precious metals (a safe haven when markets are unstable). I also allocated approximately 20 percent of my cash in a market-neutral—long and short—basket of options to take advantage of short-term opportunities.

Note the reference to "approaching" conditions. You will have to do a little bit of market anticipation; otherwise you will always be a little too late. It just takes practice. Today, alone, for example, a barrel of oil declined $10 a barrel from historic highs, absolutely killing the values of energy-related companies such as oil refineries and drillers. If you were not already short the sector you would have missed most of the opportunity to profit. By the time you witnessed the sector weakening it would have already moved. Too late. For example, I had no idea that oil would trade off $10 a barrel, but we were already short because we *anticipated* weakness. The reason is that in each of the last four months, energy rallied in the first two weeks of the month then sold off like crazy in the final five days of the month. The first two times we got hurt: the last five days of each prior month eliminated all of the profits we had earned month-to-date. Noticing the pattern, in the last two months we rode the same energy rally to the top, then midmonth bought put spreads on individual names, an energy ETF, symbol XLE. The second two months we earned more than 80 percent just for anticipating the writing on the wall.

The point is that once you trade with themes, as we discussed in chapter 4, it is important that you have more than one and that you somehow fit them all together in your portfolio. The examples above had a growth theme expressed with the weights in metals, commodities, and foreign currencies; I also had a doom theme that hedged my growth expectations.

Market themes have multiple influences on stocks, bonds, or commodities. Sometimes they combine harmoniously such that all assets perform well, and other times the influences are sufficiently disparate that your portfolio would be split sharply into winners and losers. Your challenge is to position your portfolio to benefit whether there is harmony or discord amongst market themes. One theme or another was usually getting killed while the others flourished. Together, they should be sufficiently uncorrelated that on balance you will make money.

Summary

Researchers have devoted a lot of time to thinking about exactly this phenomenon. The questions are: What makes a stock move? Why do they change in value? Are these influences constant? Can you predict them? And if you can predict these changes, can you also predict their effect on securities?

Causal influences, market "themes," that affect asset values and market movements are called factors—*market* factors. The Fave Five are primary factors, the five most influential factors, but there are as many as 128 identified market factors.[5] If you know these factors' influence on your investment targets, you will also know how their changes will influence the value of the various financial assets in your portfolio. You can thus create a portfolio of multiple factor exposures based on directional predictions. That is how you prepare for approaching market conditions. If you believe that GDP will increase in the face of continued inflation and a weak dollar, then you would position your portfolio to stocks and trades that would react favorably to higher GDP. Knowing how each of these factors would affect your potential positions is critical in composing your portfolio. When interest rates go up, certain stocks benefit—perhaps the financial sector—and others suffer, perhaps consumer discretionary. If exports are up and the dollar is down, there are cer-

---

5. Barra factor model.

tain export companies that will benefit, while companies that depend on imports may suffer.

٠ Without changes in market factors, there is no change in prices. Without a movement in prices, there are no trading profits to be had. For example, if consumption patterns never change, revenues never increase or decrease; this kind of inactivity would result in static asset prices. But every year, more people are born, we consume various goods, we travel, we want flat-screen TVs and fast cars, and we borrow money to purchase our homes and finance our educations. Change is endemic to life. Change foments volatility, and volatility foments profits. Change is good. Understanding market factors can help you predict change and preposition your portfolio.

Financial corelationships are the causal give-and-go that you can use to benefit your trading. None of these relationships is absolute because market conditions are not constant, nor do they repeat in exactly the same way. The trick is to identify your long-term themes and construct a road map for how all of the themes interrelate. The Fave Five can be instrumental in developing a set of fundamental criteria for directing your money to profitable destinations.

CHAPTER 6

DIVING DEEPER INTO THE FAVE FIVE

Referring to market themes, or market factors, we know that they have a profound effect on sectors, industries, individual securities, commodities, and so on. Now we will take a closer look at the mechanism for those influences. Let's now get specific about precisely where, in terms of investable instruments, the market factors would exert their influence.

Every company, every common stock can be categorized into one of ten possible sectors, as categorized by the Global Industry Classification Standard (GICS) defined by MSCI Barra. The investment themes you pursue will be grounded in these sectors. There are only ten. The ten GICs sectors for equities are listed below.

1. **Consumer Discretionary** represents companies that manufacture the consumer wants as opposed to consumer needs. Customer wants are discretionary in that the consumer purchases these goods to enhance their lifestyles rather than to satisfy basic needs. For that reason they are sensitive to economic cycles. Consumer Discretionary companies include car manufacturers, leisure equipment manufacturers, hotels, and restaurants. Examples are Home Depot (HD),

McDonald's (MCD), Nike (NIKE), and Time Warner (TWX).

2. **Consumer Staples** are comprised of companies that
   sell consumer needs. They are less sensitive to economic cycles—everybody's got to wear underwear,
   right? These companies manufacture and sell food/
   beverages, tobacco, prescription drugs, and house-
   hold products. Examples of consumer staples companies are Procter & Gamble (PG), Anheuser Busch
   (BUD), CVS Caremark (CVS), Kraft Foods (KFT),
   and Wal-Mart (WMT).

3. **Energy** companies sell energy or energy products,
   or provide services to energy producers, including
   oil, gas, and coal producers. The developers of oil
   rigs, drilling equipment, and other energy-related
   services and equipment are also included. Examples
   include Chevron (CVX), Devon Energy (DVN),
   National Oil Well Varco (NOV), and Schlumberger
   Ltd. (SLB).

4. **Financials** include investment banks and investment
   management companies and insurance companies.
   Other members of the Financials sector include
   commercial banks, mortgage companies, credit card
   companies, and asset management companies. Examples are American Express (AXP), American
   International Group (AIG), Wells Fargo (WFC),
   Goldman Sachs (GS), and U.S. Bancorp (USB).

5. **Health Care** sector is comprised of two industry
   groups: manufacturing and research/development.
   The manufacturers are companies who manufacture equipment and provide basic health-care services. The R&D industry group includes primarily
   the developers of pharmaceuticals and biotechnol-

ogy products. Examples include Johnson & Johnson (JNJ), Amgen (AMGN), Eli Lilly (LLY), and Medtronic (MDT).

6. **Industrials** are the companies that build the hard backbone of America. It is by far the largest sector of the GICS. Because the sector is so large and varied, some managers break this sector further down into Capital Goods and Conglomerates. The underlying industries include aerospace and defense, construction, engineering and building products, electrical equipment, and industrial machinery. The sector also covers companies that provide commercial services and supplies, including printing, employment, environmental and office services, and companies that provide transportation services (including airlines), couriers, and marine, road, and rail, and transportation infrastructure. The health of the industrials sector is considered to be a predictor of the economy's overall health. Examples include Caterpillar (CAT), Boeing (BA), Deere (DE), and Lockheed Martin (LMT).

7. **Information Technology** includes software developers, database management firms, and technology consulting and services. It also includes hardware and equipment, including communications equipment, computers and peripherals, electronic equipment, and semiconductors. Examples include Google (GOOG), Apple Computer (AAPL), 3M (MMM), and IBM (IBM).

8. **Materials** companies include those that manufacture chemicals, construction materials, glass, paper, forest products, and related packaging products; and metals (including gold, copper, silver), minerals, and

mining companies, including producers of steel. Examples include Agnico-Eagle Mines (AEM), Barrick Gold (ABX), Dow Chemical (DOW), Alcoa (AA), and U.S. Steel (X). They are generally considered to be good hedges against inflation.

9. **Telecommunications** include telephone and communications companies, including fixed line, cellular, and wireless; high-bandwidth and/or fiber-optic cable companies. Examples include Verizon (VZ), ATT (T), and Level 3 Communications (LVLT).

10. **Utilities** includes the electric, gas, and water utilities and distributors of power from alternative sources. Examples include Southern (SO), FPL Group (FPL), First Solar (FSLR), and American Electric (AEP).

Just about every company or stock, if not all, will fall into one of these ten categories. Each sector can be broken down into subgroups of industries and then actual stocks, but we are not going to go there yet. Let us be content for the moment to create a simple plan for how investment themes map onto these ten sectors. Later, we will cross-reference these ten sectors with the Fave Five market factors to see if we can create a functional road map of how to construct a hedge portfolio based on the relationship between the themes on the horizon (among them, the Fave Five) versus these ten GICS sectors.

Commodities

We know that commodities are the fuel that enable companies to run. Irrespective of the sector, every company is dependent upon commodities. The contracts to purchase commodities exist so that real operating companies can acquire the raw goods to operate and run their enterprises. There are two basic traders in commodities: the companies that need the commodity to operate, and the speculators—like you and me—who seek to profit by front-running the demand (or lack of demand) of the companies who use commodities in the course of their business. Manufacturers transact in commodities in order to conduct their businesses while speculators buy and sell commodities strictly to profit from the trends of supply and demand. Speculators do not need the commodity—they just want to sell it at a higher price to those who do. Seems kind of unfair doesn't it?

So, as a trader, commodities trading is a pure play on supply and demand. There are no underlying corporate operations to analyze, only the demand or lack of demand for commodities. Commodities include metals (such as gold, silver, platinum), grain, pork bellies, oil, and the like. The demand for or supply of commodities is directly related to the global economy and consumption.

The modern commodity markets have their roots mostly in the trading of agricultural products. Farmers would use these instruments as a way of smoothing out their revenue, securing in advance the price for which they would sell their crops. While wheat, corn, cattle, and pigs were widely traded using standard instruments in the nineteenth century in the United States, futures contracts for other basic foods, such as soybeans, were only added quite recently in most markets.

There are three general ways to trade commodities. Spot trading is any transaction in which delivery takes place immediately. Forward contracts are an agreement between two parties to exchange at some fixed future date a given quantity of a commodity for a price defined today. The fixed price today is known as the forward price. Futures contracts have the same general features as a forward contract, except that they are transacted through a futures exchange.

With each of the three types of contracts, the buyer or the

trader is buying or selling the right to acquire or deliver the physical, underlying commodity. In the spot market, such delivery is immediate. In the forward and futures markets, the delivery will occur at some future date. In all cases, the actual physical goods will be delivered to the holder of the contract. Do not ever forget that!

The prospect of physical deliveries can have comical consequences. Jig Johnson, a trader in New York, learned that lesson the hard way. He had been buying commodities furiously in anticipation of an increase in commodity prices. And so they did: Jig closed the month with a tidy profit, having gone steeply long in commodities. The stress paid off, and the profit saved his year. Jig was a fairly terrible trader, so a positive month was a welcome and rare achievement. But Jig was not the sharpest knife in the drawer, and not very organized. He sold his long positions prior to expiration, unaware that he was still long one future in heating oil. On the date of expiration, therefore, the future was exercised. A week goes by. Ring. "Yeah, hi, Mr. Johnson. We would like to make arrangements to deliver the 42,000 U.S. gallons of heating oil you bought. Can you please give us your delivery address?" "What?!" Since Jig had not sold the long future, he was now the exasperated owner of a truckload of the physical commodity—42,000 gallons of heating oil. Jig was freaked out. "Where am I going to put 42,000 gallons of heating oil?!" Yet he was obligated to take delivery by virtue of being long the expired futures contract. Frantically he hit the phones to see if he could find anyone to take it off his hands. Eventually, Jig sold the heating oil to Exxon as a spot contract, but as Exxon was aware of his situation, they significantly cut Jig on the price, no doubt giggling all the while.

On the trading floor there are all kinds of stories about how a trader goes on vacation, touring the jungles of Africa, only to come home and find 20,000 metric tons of wheat in his driveway because he forgot to sell or roll over his long futures positions. Commodities futures settle for physical delivery only and not cash, like the financial futures. It makes sense: commodities futures are designed for those companies that actually *require* delivery of the goods, not for the speculators and traders who just want to make a profit from it. The holders of the futures are obligated to take delivery, and if they are short, they are obligated to deliver.

I like the (probably fictitious) story of Rick Lubin, known as Lubie or Dick Lube, on the floor of the NYMEX exchange. The story goes that he was unaware that he was short the CME butter future.[1] Several days later he received a notification from the clearinghouse that he needs to settle the futures contract and deliver 40,000 pounds of Grade AA butter. So he ran frantically around New York, buying up all the butter cartons he could find from A&P (and other supermarkets) in order to make good on his delivery. I don't know if it's true, but it always makes me laugh. Anyway, below are the major commodities contracts:

Exchange	Contract
CBT	Wheat
CBT	Corn
CBT	Soybeans
CSC	Coffee
CSC	Sugar
CSC	Cocoa
NYC	Cotton

---

1. The Chicago Mercantile Exchange got its start as the Chicago Butter and Eggs Board.

Exchange	Contract
CME	Lean Hogs
CME	Cattle (Live)
CME	Cattle (Feeder)
NYM	Oil No 2
IPE	Oil Gasoil
NYM	Oil Unleaded
NYM	Oil WTI Crude
IPE	Oil Brent Crude
NYM	Natural Gas
LME	High Grade Primary Aluminum
LME	Copper—Grade A
LME	Lead
LME	Nickle
LME	Special High Grade Zinc
CMX	Gold
CMX	Silver

Fixed Income

Bonds, also known as fixed income, is the third and last major category to consider for our mock investment portfolio. As you know, bonds pay a fixed interest rate, which is why they are referred to as fixed income for the bondholder. The total rate of return on the bond will depend on the price you pay for it. If you pay at par, or 100 percent, case A, your return on the bond will derive from the stated coupon on the bond. If you pay less than par, case B, your total annual return will be greater than the coupon. If you pay more than par, case C, your return will be less. Assume a one-year bond pays a coupon of 5 percent. If you pay $100 for the bond, your cash return will be $5, or 5 percent; case A. If you pay $80 for the bond, your cash return will be, still, $5, for a total return of 6.25 percent; case B. If you pay $120, your total return would be 4.2 percent; case C. The coupon and the corresponding price paid for the bond is a reflection of the credit quality of the issuing party and prevailing market interest rates.

Bonds are about as diverse as equities. Every publicly traded company will usually have at least one bond offering that is publicly traded. Whether the company's bonds or stocks appear attractive to you as an investor will depend on your risk preferences and the current markets. Hedge managers who "trade the balance sheet" not only buy and sell the equity, the common stock, of a company but also they will trade its debt. As with the Bear Stearns acquisition, for example, hedge managers bought the debt (because it was selling at cents on the dollar, much less than $100 and later ostensibly guaranteed by the Fed) and shorted the stock for a double windfall when Bear ran into trouble.

Bonds fall into three main categories: corporate debt, municipal debt, and sovereign debt. Corporate debt is issued by publicly traded companies. Municipal debt is issued by local governments. Sovereign debt is issued by national governments.

In all three cases, the credit quality of the issuing entity (company, local municipality, or nation) will determine the relative interest rate of one bond to another. For example, the sovereign debt of developed nations carries a lower interest rate than that of developing nations as a result of differences in perceived risk. The debt of the United Kingdom returns, for example, 5 percent for a five-year bond versus a 10 percent coupon for a five-year note from Brazil. The lower-risk nation—the United Kingdom—carries a lower interest rate. The same is true of corporations that issue debt. Corporations pay higher interest if their credit quality is low and lower interest if their credit quality is high. Companies that are well run are rewarded by being able to borrow cheaply.

The yield curve—the change in interest rate relative to the change in bond maturity—is shown below as a line that illustrates the market interest rates for bonds of different maturities. Generally, the longer the term of the bond, the higher the interest rate will be. Nonetheless, there are periods when these relationships invert usually signalling secular change in the economy. The yield curve can flatten, steepen, or invert (i.e., par for short duration bonds is at, below, or above 100, respectively) based on economic conditions. And such movements—like most volatility—represent a great trading opportunity.

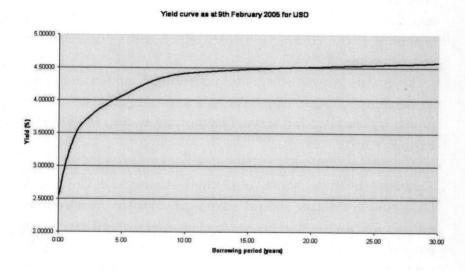

The yield curve above illustrates that a five-year bond in the open markets would yield approximately 4 percent, while a thirty-year loan would yield roughly 4.7 percent. That 70–basis-point difference, or 0.7 percent, between the five-year and thirty-year yields, is a fairly tight spread.

Your Co-relationship System

Let us set up a simple system comprised of two groups: on the one hand we have the Fave Five, and on the other, we have stocks, bonds, and commodities. How do they fit with one another? How can these interrelationships result in good trades?

Fave One: Changes in GNP

If the country were a company, Gross National Product (GNP) would be the top-line revenue. GNP represents revenue before expenses. It is the sum of every transaction that occurs in the country. The most important attribute of the GNP for your purposes is whether it is lesser or greater than the last time it was reported. Increases are good for the economy, because they indicate growth in business activity, profits and share value; and decreases indicate a contraction in the economy. If the contraction is sustained it may be classified as a recession.

Economic growth stimulates consumer confidence: people spend more, companies sell more, and profits increase. When profits increase, cash reserves (savings) grow, and the world is generally better off.

Growth in GNP raises all boats, so most sectors should have a positive outlook, some more than others. The Consumer Discretionary sector should have quite positive reactions to economic growth—but not every consumer discretionary *company* within the sector will fare well. Management and relative competitive performance will be a large determinant of how a company performs within a sector, relative to its peers. Find the sectors that express your performance plan then find the companies within the sector that will capture it best. Good longs are companies that tend to have high earnings growth rates and dominant competitive positions whereas good shorts tend to be companies with deteriorating fundamentals and/or poor competitive positions.

In terms of business-cycle fundamentals, a billion-dollar business is no different than a small business, such as a restaurant in your neighborhood. When things are great, the tables are full. Customers are ordering dessert, buying an extra glass of wine, and splurging on bottles of sparkling water. Revenue is up, and so are profits. In the stock market, that results in higher prices for your stock.

When the economy is soft, the tables are empty, customers are ordering only appetizers, food stock sometimes spoils for lack of demand, and sometimes the costs of operations is greater than revenues. In that scenario, the business is not throwing off any cash and, as a result, has a lesser value.

My objective is to buy sectors that are growing faster than the overall market, then find companies that are dominant within those sectors. Getting the right GICS sectors is most of the game. Finding the right stocks within a sector is the next important step. Attractive companies within a sector may be identified by a low price/earnings to growth (PEG) ratio.

The PEG ratio is an elegant measure of value because it examines the current earnings yield of a company and compares that yield to future growth expectations. Low PEG ratios on growth companies in strong sectors may be a leading indicator of future accelerated price advancement. A relatively low PEG could mean that the stock is undervalued. The absolute value of the PEG ratio is less important than the value of a company's PEG ratio relative to its peers.

I look to short sell companies whose prices have exceeded their current growth prospects. Sometimes short trades consist of companies that were once great long targets, but the market overshot reasonable levels in a gush of irrational exuberance. Other attractive short prospects are companies in sectors or industries subject to disruptive technologies (such as Polaroids versus digital photos or America Online versus Al Gore's Internet). Short prospects may also include companies with deteriorating fundamentals, i.e., companies that aren't doing so great, as evidenced by declining profit margins or revenue growth, such as Ford or Agilent Technologies. In the case of Agilent, the company has missed analysts' earnings estimates in eight of the last nine quarters by a very wide margin. In the event that I cannot find good shorts, I will short the entire market (the S&P 500) using index futures (or e-minis for the individual) or buy the ETF UltraShort Dow30 ProShares (DXD). The DXD is a really cool ETF. It *increases* in value by two times for each unit that the Dow Jones Industrials Index *decreases*. It is a short position that you can actually buy *and* get 2 to 1 leverage. You can also buy the UltraShort S&P 500 ProShares (SDS).

To illustrate this point, below is the rationale for a trade I made in August 2007 based on the changes in Gross National Product, Fave Five #1.

I bought Deere & Co. long for the following reasons:

Deere is an agricultural equipment maker that is dominant in the Agricultural sector. The company's stock was trading at a discount to the S&P 500 in that it carried a price/earnings (P/E) ratio and a PEG ratio substantially less than the S&P 500. Due to the demand for commodities the sector was strong, indicating that Deere's price growth was far more likely to accelerate upward than to slow down. Deere is the world's largest maker of farm equipment, which accounts for more than 50 percent of companywide revenues. Its other operations include forestry and housing products. Deere's major sales occur in the United States and other developed countries, which, thanks to the ethanol push and the demand for food, had profits growing nicely. My theory supporting a buy was that as developing countries (increasing GNP) shift to centralized farming, the demand for farm equipment would surge. That would benefit the sector but would particularly benefit Deere. Its stock price was already selling at a discount to the sector (as measured by the PEG), so the upside potential was great.

A quick word on the other asset classes. In terms of GNP, if economic activity is robust, then bond prices generally increase and yields decline. Easy money, or low-interest-rate environments, generally fuel greater economic activity. It becomes easier for businesses to buy the equipment and property necessary to run operations, and it enables consumers to borrow to make their "want" purchases in addition to their "need" purchases. In terms of bonds versus stocks, some traders compare the one-year return on bonds to the real dividend yield on the S&P 500. If the bond yield is higher, they start to be relatively attractive compared to stocks and warrant higher portfolio allocation.

What does the GNP mean for commodities? The consumption of commodities is derivative of the health of the global economy, and the strength of the dollar—not just of the U.S. economy. As we have noted, commodities, unlike stocks, are a pure play of supply and demand. Commodities are simply goods purchased by companies so they can go about their course of business. Whether great companies demand commodity purchases or poor companies demand commodity purchases, the demand leads to increased commodity prices. Therefore, GNP and commodity prices are usually positively correlated. The caveat is that commodities are in demand globally. U.S. GNP, while important, is not singularly responsible for demand or price pressures in commodities.

Fave Two: Consumer Confidence

Confidence in the economy and the capital markets is a key driver of market fluctuations and the business cycle. When consumer confidence increases, consumers want to buy stuff. When confidence decreases, people want to buy less stuff. Therefore, consumer confidence is a forerunner of changes in the economy and therefore in the markets. If consumers feel great, economic activity increases, companies profit, and stock prices rise—particularly for consumer-oriented companies. If consumer confidence erodes, economic activity decreases, companies profit less, and stock prices decline, especially for cyclical or consumer-sensitive companies. Consumers are less likely to purchase nonessential items, such as flat-screen TVs, perfume, and Chia Pets.

I recently made a trade on such a phenomenon. It happened to be an idea upon which Jim Cramer concurred and commented. Technology was hit really hard in the first quarter of 2008. Many of the consumer-related stocks were hurt because of the strong possibility of a recession. When Apple hit $119, I was already interested, just based on its fundamental ratios. But when the government announced that it would issue rebate checks to Americans to help get through the rough period, I bought Apple. Jim Cramer thought similarly, suggesting at the time that the $600–per-person stimulus from the government was going to go right to discretionary purchases, such as iPods. This was a speculative trade, so I did not buy the stock, but I purchased a 125/140 call spread on Apple stock. It took a few weeks, but eventually like-minded traders pushed the stock over $140. I did well.

At the same time, from an existing position from 2007, I shorted Palm Inc. (PALM). Palm is a mobile computing, manufacturer making products including Palm Treo smartphones, Palm LifeDrive Mobile Managers, and Palm handheld computers, as well as software, services, and accessories. I like the industry a lot. But I didn't like the company.

Shares of Palm seemed expensive given the competitive landscape and the company's then-recent profit results. Shares were trading at more than fifty times forward earnings, and with earnings growth estimated at 10 to 12 percent, the stock was expensive on a PEG basis as well compared to the S&P 500 (around 1.8). In the summer of 2007, Palm was a company facing a major rival in Research In Motion (RIMM), which had a very successful growth spurt because of the BlackBerry. Its nickname, "crackberry," is testimony to its comparative popularity. On top of that, Palm was facing a formidable new rival in Apple, who had launched its wildly popular iPhone. The iPhone was a phenomenon, alone responsible for a 40 percent increase in Apple's market share of the desktop computer market. I sold Palm short at $15 per share and held it short for almost nine months. As of this writing, the stock is trading at $5 per share, for a profit of over 60 percent. This is a great example of how two companies can sit on opposite sides of a strong sector, providing a hedge opportunity.

Changes in GNP and consumer confidence are kissing cousins. Declines in consumer confidence can result in declines in GNP, as consumers decrease their spending. Keep this in mind—historically, *90 percent* of all economic rebounds are led by increases in consumer confidence. Consumers, in the end, are a primary driver of consumption. When they are confident, that generally has a positive impact on the economy.

Fave Three: Expectations on Interest Rates

Are you thinking to yourself that the Fave Five are interrelated? Right you are. Changes in expectations on interest rates will significantly affect the markets, too—stocks and bonds more than commodities.

There are many factors that effect a change in interest rates. One of the most important is the monetary policy of the central bank (of any developed nation) and whether it is tightening (raising interest rates) or easing (lowering interest rates). In most economic environments, a reduction in interest rates is a stimulus for economic activity. As a result of the decrease in the "cost" of money, companies will borrow more to make investments, acquire machinery, hire personnel, and increase production. Lower borrowing costs also boost consumer confidence, which further fuels economic activity. The reverse is true if interest rates increase.

But interest rates are not a perfect stimulator of stocks. The Fed's powerful hammer—monetary policy—can only go so far. There are many other factors that bear on stocks, so interest rates do not correspond strictly with the movements in the stock market. Since August 2007 for example, the Fed has moved aggressively to cut rates to create liquidity and stimulate economic activity (some say too late: check youtube.com "Cramer: Bernanke, Wake Up," or "Every Breath Bernanke Takes"). Below is a graph relating the interest-rate changes to the stock market changes. It is fairly strong evidence that lower interest rates spur stock market growth.

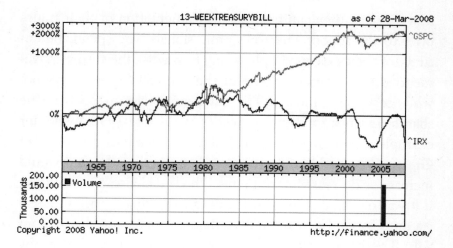

GSPC = S&P 500, IRX = 3–month Treasury rates

Generally, expectations on interest rates going up will decrease stock and bond prices (and as a result, increase the yield on the bonds purchased). There are two reasons. Higher interest rates increase the cost of borrowing for companies, so it simply costs more to do business. Their customers are also affected by higher interest rates, which affects the consumers' bottom line and encroaches on their ability to make purchases. Higher interest rates directly affect the consumer, too. You have likely heard often about the mountain of debt sitting on consumers' shoulders that may prove troublesome for the economy. Consumers saddled with high credit card debt eventually have to start paying it off, which makes it less likely that they will have discretionary money to spend—even less likely if interest rates rise.

Conversely, expectations on interest rates going down will increase stock and bond prices. Note the use of term "interest rate expectations." Expectation plays a very large role in the movement of both stocks and bonds. Traders seek to anticipate the move so that they can time the implementation of their trades prior to the action. There are professionals who spend the entirety of their careers simply trying to predict the future movement of interest rates. Some of the methodologies are sound, while others are amusing. There was an analyst on CNNfn (the shameless stock market cheerleader in the late 1990s) who, for example, depending on the size of the briefcase carried by Alan Greenspan, would attempt to predict whether the Fed would increase or decrease interest rates. The Fed chairman's briefcase, if it was bursting at its seams, would indicate a change in interest rates. A flat briefcase indicated no action—or so the wisdom was. The briefcase method was not very accurate, but in any case Alan Greenspan got wind of it—CNNfn would broadcast pictures of the chairman's briefcase on the mornings of Federal Open Market Committee meetings, after all—and started to leave his paperwork at home. For the average investor, nonetheless, there is plenty of predictive value in the daily newspapers and Internet blogs. For better or worse, Ben Bernanke, the chairman of the Federal Reserve, has been far more communicative than Greenspan, so there has been less guesswork required by the market with respect to direction on rates.

Some sectors and companies may benefit in a high-interest-rate environment. The Financials sector benefits even in a high-interest-rate environment because they can pass the cost of higher interest rates on to the customer. In passing the cost on to the consumer, financial institutions are also able to sneak in higher profit margins. ABC bank borrows at one rate (in the form of offering CDs and savings accounts to ordinary depositors) and lends at a higher rate to other borrowers (such as mortgagors and commercial borrowers). The difference between the two is called the debit/credit spread. You may notice it in your own brokerage account. The broker pays you one rate on your idle cash and another rate for you to borrow to purchase shares on margin. The difference can be 4 percentage points(!) or more. The costs will increase if interest rates rise, because banks and brokerages have to pay a higher rate to depositors. They are able to lend at a higher rate, however, and they tend to accelerate the increase of the debit/credit spread as interest rates rise, increasing their profits.

When a trader trades a bond, meaning that he does not intend to hold it for an extended period, it is because he anticipates a movement in the bond price due to a change in interest rates. Remember the cases A, B, and C we calculated earlier? Well, if interest rates go from 6.25 percent to 4.20 percent, that would result in a profit on the bond of 50 percent, from $80 to $120, if you were already holding the bond. And that return is without leverage! In reality, movements in bond prices are generally much subtler than that, but you get the picture.

Bond trading can be highly leveraged, so a little loss goes a long way. Bond traders can also get killed if they bet the wrong way. John Meriwether's fixed-income hedge fund, JWM Partners Inc., for example, was down 24 percent in the first quarter of 2008, as the Fed aggressively lowered rates. He is not alone, however, just famous.

Faves Four and Five: Short-Term and Long-Term Inflationary Expectations

Inflation can be nasty. We have not had a real, hard dose of inflation since the 1970s. For more than two decades, we have had a unique period of unprecedented economic growth combined with low interest rates and low inflation. This cocktail of high growth and low inflation has created a great deal of wealth. But inflation does creep up, like now, so you should be wary of its consequences.

The hyperinflation that sometimes occurs in the emerging markets is an extreme example. Living in Zimbabwe, one could go to the market and buy bread on a Monday for $1 and on Friday it could cost $2. Next week it could be $4—and you still have to feed your family. The developed world has not often seen hyperinflation, but the 1970s was close enough. In Zimbabwe, the annual rate of inflation is more than 5,000 percent. By the end of the year, that same loaf of bread could cost $50 for that matter. Other nations that have experienced hyperinflation and the ruin it can cause include Brazil, Argentina, and Peru in the 1980s and Russia in the mid-1990s. The bare food shelves were a stark illustration of inflation's ruinous reach. When inflation begins to show, markets worry and necessarily reposition their portfolios for defensive protection.

The causes of inflation are many. One is a result of the amount of debt a nation may owe and the ongoing need to borrow to sustain the economy. As of March 2008, for example, the total U.S. federal debt was approximately $9.4 trillion, about $79,000 on average for each American taxpayer.[2] Private debt, mortgage debt, and credit cards are even higher, at $11 trillion, weighing down the American taxpayer even further. When Americans borrow to sustain the U.S. economy or even borrow in their private lives, it decreases their ability to make future purchases without an increase in real wages or income. And that impairs future GNP. The way the Fed fights the financial squeeze is basically to print more money for consumers to spend.

And so it is. Easy access to money is a direct cause of inflation. As a direct result of America's borrowing to sustain itself, the U.S. dollar is flying overseas in interest payments to our creditors—now nearing $700 billion a year, driving the dollar to record lows against the euro and the yen. Eventually, Asians

---

2. Wikipedia, United States Public Debt entry.

and Europeans will stop spending their profits on U.S. Treasury bonds.

"Inflation is worse even than a depression" according to Stephen Leeb, author of *The Coming Economic Collapse: How You Can Thrive When Oil Costs $200 a Barrel* and *Game Over: How the Collapsing Economy Will Sink Wealth by 50% or More—Unless You Know What to Do*. "As a smart investor, you can handle a depression. But inflation can be devastating."

1930s versus the 1970s[3]

For the decade of the 1930s, the total real returns were:

Stocks (S&P 500): +21.9%
Cash: +29.3%
Bonds: +94.9%

For the inflationary decade of the 1970s, the total real returns were:

Stocks (S&P 500): -14.0%
Cash: -10.5%
Bonds: -17.5%

There are tactics, however, for protecting against inflation. The onslaught of inflation is sufficiently slow that you can easily prepare and switch your money into those few investments that actually profit from inflation. For example, in chapter 4, we drew a graph of inflation protected notes (IPNs) versus the stock market. The IPNs gained significantly as inflation crept up relative to the stock market, clearly showing the benefit of hedging against inflation with IPNs.

---

3. The Complete Investor.

You can also invest in markets that are not suffering from inflation or whose growth is outpacing that of the United States. Anyone can easily trade out of dollars by going to the local bank, and participate in foreign currency markets through hard, physical currency. You can also invest in U.S. companies with a global presence. For many U.S. multinational companies, such as Coca-Cola or General Electric, their revenue streams from overseas markets are significant. Their stocks represent a hedge to inflation since their performance is based on markets other than our own. Multinationals benefit from sales in multiple currencies, especially those that are strong or appreciating versus the U.S. dollar. You can also purchase country level ETFs. Let the experts running the ETF figure out how best to exploit those foreign markets; you just benefit from their performance.

Another great hedge against inflation is gold. Precious metals are great hedges. To me, gold has dubious value[4] as a shiny and pretty metal, but the reality is that gold has been one of the investments proven to be a safe haven in the face of inflation. In the 1970s, a time of double-digit inflation in the United States, the price of gold rose at an average annualized rate of 33 percent a year, representing a better than ninefold gain in actual purchasing power. Gold has historically been a very strong counter to inflation and a great hedge in any portfolio.

Given gold's anticorrelation with inflation, advances in gold prices can be a leading indicator of inflation. Between 1970 and 1974, for example, as inflation rose into double digits, gold outperformed other commodities by more than 2 to 1. More important, gold started its move in 1971–1972—before inflation

---

4. Gold "gets dug out of the ground in Africa, or someplace. Then we melt it down, dig another hole, bury it again and pay people to stand around guarding it. It has no utility. Anyone watching from Mars would be scratching their head."—Warren Buffett

really took off, which implies that it is both a leading indicator of inflation and a hedge to inflation. Commodity prices tend to precede inflation because it takes time for the higher cost of raw materials prices to work their way through the economy. For example, oil hit an all-time high in 2008, over $110 a barrel, but the economy was still growing modestly, at an annual rate of 1 percent. Eventually, oil would increase the cost of living by increasing the cost of virtually everything, from food, to clothes, to transportation, to labor, resulting in observed inflation and threatening a recession to boot.[5]

Here is a quick story about gold's ability to retain its value over time. A good friend of mine, a very successful global macro trader, was having trouble in his marriage. He led an idyllic life. He lived in tony East Hampton with his family in a twenty-room mansion he affectionately called "the Palace." He commuted to New York three days a week, some days by chauffeur, and others by helicopter. Monday, Friday, and the weekends he would spend his time in East Hampton. He and his wife had only one child, a precocious boy, age seven.

His marriage started to fall apart because he was highly driven in his career, probably to excess. Eighteen-hour days six days a week paid for a lot of Chanel, a great collection of cars, and a home in Saint Barthelemy, but it left his wife sufficiently alone that she learned to live without him. At first she grieved over her loneliness, then she pleaded, then she became angry, and then she plotted. She decided to leave him.

Once she informed him of the spin-off, he had only moments to retrieve whatever he needed to survive offsite—potentially for quite some time. While he gathered his things, he recalled in an "aha!" moment that he had stashed gold ingots in his personal safe. He retrieved them, which was a good

---

5. The Complete Investor.

thing, because all of the bank accounts were then frozen in anticipation of a spin-off of equals. Anyway, as we sipped beer and recounted both the good and bad times and his grief, we both remarked "thank God gold holds it value and is a liquid currency." He had stashed away a cache of gold in 1985 and dusted it off for more than three times that amount in 2008. If he had socked away cash, it would have had a today buying power of probably half or less. Gold proved itself a safe haven when hell did break loose. We washed down our T-bones with Stellas and laughed at how beautifully ridiculous life can be.

There are also new financial instruments that specifically target inflation, such as the Treasury Inflation-Protected Securities, or TIPS (ETF: TIP), which was introduced by the U.S. Department of the Treasury in 1997 as a new class of government debt obligation. The key feature of TIPS is that the payments to investors adjust automatically to compensate for the actual change in the Consumer Price Index (CPI). Conventional Treasury securities, in contrast, do not provide such protection.

The Springboard to Your Own System

The Fave Five are indispensable for getting a quick read on how to position your hedged portfolio. I have shared with you a few anecdotes and a few trade ideas here, but in the end, it will be you who has to develop your own recognition of economic patterns and market opportunities. If you track the ten sectors we have discussed and cross them with the five major market factors, the Fave Five, you will develop your own sense of how things move. Movement equals opportunity for profit. If you are there ahead of time, that movement opportunity turns into profit realization. There is no "new" magic with a hedge strategy—besides a few basic differences in leverage, short selling, and investment universe. The identification of opportunity is not unlike the traditional methods you already know. Get the sectors right, long and short, and the rest will follow.

I remember many years ago, as a young intern, I would overhear guys at Morgan Stanley in active discussions about the levels of GNP or the inflation rate or whatever. I admit that, at the time, I thought they were boring ninnies. How could they talk about such boring and meaningless data . . . *from memory*!?

"So not cool," I thought. But it is these very data—your knowledge of these factors and how they drive value—that will enable you to develop opportunities for yourself on both sides of the market, long and short. By having a feel for what drives asset prices up or down, you are in a position to construct hedge portfolios that are profitable and able to withstand broad market whimsy. And occasionally, if you want a free peek to see if you are on the money with your thinking, take a look at www.stockpickr.com or www.capitaliq.com to see what the rest of the market is thinking.

CHAPTER 7

DATA!

or,

HOW TO USE BASIC DATA IF YOU WANT TO, OR GET AROUND IT IF YOU DON'T

Every market opportunity will derive from analyzing data. If you are going to trade intelligently, you cannot avoid crunching some data, so you may as well get used to the idea that your hedge strategy will involve some level of quantitative work. That probably sounds like a drag. But intrinsic to every great investment idea is the constraint of expressing that idea at the right *price*. It is critical to assess your market ideas not only by theme but also by the price level, as in "at what valuation am I willing to pay for this opportunity?" You need to be able to determine the acceptable range for entering a trade. It better be the right price, or you are liable to lose money. A carton of Häagen-Dazs still tastes great at $10 a pint, but that same pint tastes a whole lot sweeter at $3.

Great companies do not always trade at great prices. Gerald Levin, the former CEO of Time Warner, can attest to that in regard to his ill-fated and now-infamous acquisition of AOL. Given Time Warner's competitive position, its ownership of voluminous content, and its lack of online presence, the acquisition was actually a brilliant idea. Levin simply paid too much. "This acquisition has most definitely qualified as a disaster of belly flop proportions, which *Fortune* dubbed as 'one of the greatest train wrecks in corporate history.'" As a result of the profligate overpayment for AOL, Time Warner's stock dropped 75 percent after the acquisition. The acquisition of AOL was the financial equivalent of paying $100 for a cup of coffee—the diner kind, not the Starbucks kind.

Quantitative analysis will help determine the viability of your trade ideas. I am not suggesting any techniques that would be considered abstruse. Just number-crunching a few financial ratios, like the PEG ratio, will go a long way. The alternative is to trade blindly because someone else "said so." Jim Cramer, for example, is an interesting character with a range of good ideas and some not-so-good ideas. He is a successful ex–hedge fund trader and one of the most colorful financial commentators on TV. But his opinions are, after all, info-tainment. It is better to cultivate and refine your own ideas. You are better off vetting your own decisions so that when your positions need attention—as they *inevitably* will—you don't have to rely on Jim to bail you out. You need to develop your own sense of appropriate entry points and exit points for your trades. Without a grasp of the data, that's hard to do.

If you use some basic data analysis techniques, your conclusions will not be far from what the professionals recommend. I promise. In fact, your sense of when to enter and exit a trade may be even better than that of the so-called experts. Alas, it is just not possible to make the millions you desire without crunching numbers. Wealth creation takes some work and some study. Ask any of the guys at the top of their game. Their lives appear glamorous, but I can assure you that hedge managers spend a lot of time absorbing and crunching information, trying to gain an edge in full sight of all the competition. There are no shortcuts. Imagine all the investors worldwide, bug-eyed, who are investing and armed with insightful data. How can you compete with them?

I admit that there are *some* shortcuts. You can definitely benefit from the work of others. Luckily, much of the data/conclusions that traders/analysts both use and generate is available online for free. Much of the heavy lifting has been done for you. The data are ubiquitous, so your hardest task is to make the decision, for any security, whether to buy it, short it, or do nothing. Thus, you need not weight anyone's online opinion or Web blog advice above your own because the opinions attained for free are usually worth the price you pay for them: nothing. It is hard data you should be interested in—financial ratios, operating performance data, macroeconomic observations, etc.—not opinions. If the underlying company (stocks, bonds) or commodity or currency is publicly traded, then its financial attributes are in the public domain. The information is free, accurate, and valuable.

When I started out, I kept my own database of macroeconomic statistics because then it was not possible to just log on to a site and download historical data. I collected the closing prices of a wide range of stocks as well as basic financial and macroeconomic data. I did it because I always wanted to be able to graph the financial data at a moment's notice to get a real picture of what was going on. Today that information is just a click away on reuters.com, finance.yahoo.com, stockpickr.com, and a host of other financial Web sites. Just Google "free market data."

In the old days, the 1980s, personal computers were not yet common on the desktop. There were even a few analysts I worked with who preferred to use an abacus. True! I actually did work with two Chinese analysts who liked to use an abacus instead of the ubiquitous Hewlett Packard HP-12C calculator. They were so good with their abaci that they could calculate a result faster than we could on the calculators! We once had a late-night competition between one of the Chinese analysts and the fastest hand at the HP-12C (that would be me), and for long series of calculations, he had the result before I did!

At that time, there was no Internet, at least not as we know it today. I grew up as a trader in an era when data were not readily available. We spent hours upon hours scouring the hard copies of annual reports and transcribing the data to accounting tablets so that we could quickly access the data later if we needed to. If we wanted to do a time-series analysis, a series of historical data observed for trend information (and other statistical measures), we had to somehow locate a history of annual reports and transcribe the numbers ourselves. It was long and tedious work.

In fact, that is how the analyst programs at the major investment banks began. The analyst programs were an efficient way to assemble a team of very bright college graduates, at low cost, to do all of the unglamorous calculation and analysis necessary to do investment banking transactions. The banks hired the best and brightest students right out of college from the top schools and then asked them to do what amounted to secretarial work: cull financial data from corporate annual reports; write, print, and assemble presentations; type letters; enter financial data into Excel spreadsheets for transaction analysis; or pretty much any task that would make life easier for the senior principals. Anything. There was an annual class of "freshmen" dedicated to these tasks. The banks were able to hire young analysts cheaply, relative to the value they created for the banks. Depending on the analyst, he or she would pretty soon be able to run a transaction solo, from beginning to end. The banks converted a cost of thousands of dollars for the analyst into millions of dollars in fee income for the investment bank.

Because the analysts were "best of breed," the bright-eyed novitiates could be counted on to get things right the first time and rarely, if ever, submit work that was inaccurate or incomplete. Plus, the banks would get an early look at talent that could be invited, one day, to become a partner. For the young analyst, the job meant long, long hours. But it gave a taste of what it would be like to be a real Wall Street player.

When I was an analyst at Morgan Stanley, it was very rare to leave the office before 1:00 a.m. I was in demand because I had developed a particular strength in building valuation models for companies on the "newfangled" desktop computer instead of accounting tablets. I was twenty-two years old, and as youthful exuberance would have it, I was also attending medical school at the same time. Morgan was still a privately held company and that had an impact on our culture from the top down. I could not wait to go to work. I was surrounded by very smart people whom I liked and considered friends. That we spent our time structuring transactions was almost secondary. We were having fun! I was frustrated if I did not have sufficient work to keep me at the office well into the night. I saw such freedom as an indication of their perception of my capabilities. I remember once being in the thick of a transaction and darting to the elevator at 5:00 p.m. to go buy my lunch (and breakfast) at a nearby delicatessen.[1] "Slackers," I thought to myself looking around in the crowded elevator on the way down. "They do not have the privilege to work on deals past 5:00 p.m. I am lucky."

---

1. The deli was gross. I will never forget that I once saw the cashier cleaning under his nails with the free plastic forks and placing them back in the bin. It was shut down several times by the Health Department, but it was close by and convenient.

No matter how late the night, we would have to return to the office by 8:00 a.m., six to seven days a week. Our salaries were good—except when you calculated them on an hourly basis. I would be ecstatic if I got out of the office by, say, 11:00 p.m. If I did get out "early," I would gleefully ring up all my friends and suggest meeting for a drink. Mostly, they would hang up. No one could believe that anyone could work so much and so late all of the time.

The good ol' days of toiling over numbers are long gone. According to Thomas Friedman in *The World Is Flat*, even number crunching is now outsourced. Why have the promising young recruits stay long nights to crunch numbers when one could outsource it to India for pennies on the dollar?

As a result of the Web, the new breed of crunchers, and the availability of data, today's investor has been significantly empowered. This means you can generate your own ideas with greater insight—or at least with as much data as you can possibly consume. It cuts both ways though—the consequence is greater competition. In the accounting tablet days, competition was weeded out by our access to data that was difficult to attain or create. Only a handful of market players had access to key market data, and they made a lot of money for the advantage. With access available to all, the easy opportunities have been fewer and harder to find.

Fifteen to twenty years ago, you could ostensibly print money (profits) by using a simple trend-following model such as a MACD (Moving Average Convergence/Divergence)[2] model to drive your buy and sell signals. In fact, many of the early global macro traders earned their reputations and wealth

---

2. Developed by Gerald Appel, Moving Average Convergence/Divergence (MACD) is one of the simplest indicators available to direct trade signals. MACD uses moving averages, lagging indicators, to provide insights into trend-following entry and exit points for traders.

doing exactly that. Well, unfortunately, such models do not work anymore. The world caught up. The availability of data and dissemination of "intelligence" meant that too many people had figured out how to game the MACD opportunity to their benefit. There are traders who still use MACD, but they are the guys with 30 percent annual volatility—up 30 percent one month and down 50 percent the next. The volatility is high because everybody knows the trade.

Data is ubiquitous, so that if you are not employing it, you are at a significant disadvantage. With the increase in data quality, trading models have become increasingly sophisticated, fast, and smart. Quicker access to clean data than the competition potentially uncovers a mispricing, a hidden trend, a hidden arbitrage. For example, Michael Milken was a data jockey, an early arbitrageur who virtually invented the institutional market for junk debt, an opportunity uncovered by insightful data analysis. Milken found that the prices and yields on junk debt were out of line with the actual occurrence of default. In other words, the market priced the bonds like it expected the worst, but the worst came with such infrequency that he showed that there should be a deeper market for subprime debt (sound familiar?). As a senior executive at Drexel Burnham Lambert, he created a huge market for these instruments and made a mint doing it. By the 1980s, Milken personally earned a salary estimated to be $550 million a year. In the meantime, he created some of the most competitive, fastest-growing companies of the time. When the banks ran into problems in the 1970s and turned off the capital spigot (sound familiar?), Milken stepped forward and made capital available to thousands of dynamic, growing companies that created jobs and shareholder value. He backed such pioneers as Bill McGowan (telecommunications), Craig McCaw (cellular telephones), Steve Wynn (resorts), Len Riggio (book retailing), and Bob

Toll (homebuilding), among many other leaders of the more than three thousand companies he financed.[3] These opportunities were all based on data insights and a recognition that the market wasn't getting it "right."

Alas, Milken went to jail because some of his practices were seen as illegal. The government accused Milken of bribing the managers of junk-bond funds to invest in Drexel offerings, of parking securities to claim illegal tax losses, and of engaging in insider trading and then obstructing justice by destroying documents at Drexel after the government inquiry began.[4] Milken was indicted by a federal grand jury on ninety-eight counts of fraud, racketeering, and securities violations in 1989. In a plea bargain arrangement, Milken pleaded guilty to six lesser felony counts. He was sentenced to ten years in prison and forced to pay a total of $650 million in fines and restitution but was released after less than two years.[5] In terms of constructing a strategy based on data insights, however, he was a genius. Knowing the data was powerful.

Data, Graphs, and Judgment

The best data can be expensive, but the costs have come way down. The standard issue on Wall Street is the Bloomberg Terminal, which has every piece of data you can imagine, as well as Bloomberg University, a comprehensive database of useful lessons. A Bloomberg Terminal will cost about $1,500 per month with a two-year commitment.

For most newbie traders a Bloomberg is overkill, however useful it might prove to be. An alternative is another excel-

3. www.michaelmilken.com.
4. *New York Times*, "Full Scope of Inquiry Into Milken, Kurt Eichenwald," September 26, 1990.
5. Dan G. Stone, *April Fools: An Insider's Account of the Rise and Collapse of Drexel Burnham*.

lent product: Reuters BridgeStation. Not quite as convenient as Bloomberg in terms of its user interface, it still has just as much, if not more, data. It's also much cheaper than the Bloomberg Terminal (approximately $300 per month) and is available on the Internet.

I believe that the most comprehensive free financial site on the Web is finance.yahoo.com. You can use it for free on any computer with an Internet connection and you can get everything you need to know and more. I use it myself when I don't have access to my own resources. The Yahoo! site has data for every asset class there is. The market data is delayed twenty minutes, which should not be an issue for most investors and for $9.95 per month, you can get real-time data.

I am amazed at how much data has been made available on the Internet to the average investor. You have to understand that twenty years ago, access to this kind of data was the sole reason that the best traders dominated the industry. They simply had better and more data than anyone else. They had a real edge as a result. Now that same kind of data is available to you. It only takes a few clicks to assemble the data to test any market theory you can think of.

If going quantitative is not your strong suit, don't fret. While I believe that quantitative analysis is the lifeblood of good ideas, it is certainly possible to conduct an "analysis" of quantitative data by looking at graphs. Tracking historical *changes* in financial data—i.e., a financial chart—can be worth a million words.

Let me show you what I mean. Let us take a look at a series of financial data charts, comprised of the daily closing prices of select securities. The first chart will contain only one series. For each successive chart, we will add another data series. The purpose is to demonstrate how you can use the power of graphical data to make conclusions in the absence of hard data or number crunching.

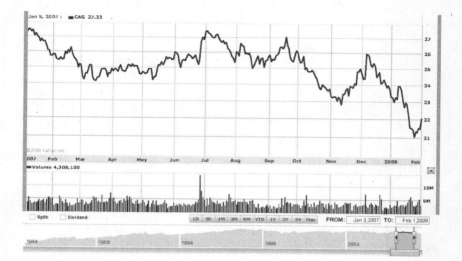

In 2007, ConAgra Foods (CAG), price chart above, earned a $300 million profit from commodities trading compared to a normal trading return of $100 million, historically. ConAgra is a member of the Agriculture sector, so futures trading in commodities was not a core business. ConAgra's core business is manufacturing and distributing packaged food, but commodities trading was a necessary and profitable ancillary business. Usually, investors do not reward a company for noncore ancillary business activity, but the trading of commodities futures is endemic to the agricultural business. That ConAgra made a fairly large profit at it was icing on the cake. But compared to Deere (DE), the capital appreciation of ConAgra stock was paltry—reflected by its change in price over the period.

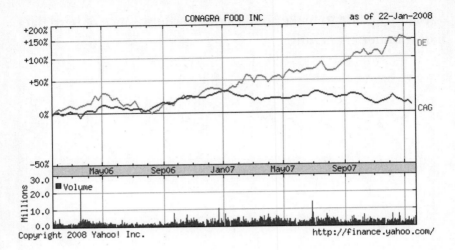

Looking at the comparative historical price graph, what can you say about the opportunity here?

First, ConAgra and Deere are companies belonging to the same GICS sector, Industrial Goods, but note that they are not in the same industry. An Industry is a subset of the Sector and describes the primary business of the company in greater detail. ConAgra's industry is Packaged Goods; Deere's is Farm and Construction Machinery. In recent years, ConAgra changed its business model from the production of commodities (such as grain, protein, pork, beef, and chicken) to the manufacturing of packaged foods (such as Orville Redenbacher's, Chef Boyardee, Healthy Choice, Marie Callender's, Slim Jim, Hebrew National, and so on).

Deere is known for the production of the equipment necessary for agribusiness, operating in four segments: agricultural equipment, commercial and consumer equipment, smaller units in construction and forestry, and credit. The agricultural equipment segment offers a line of farm equipment and related service parts, including tractors; combine, cotton, and sugarcane harvesters; tillage, seeding, and soil preparation machinery; and so on.

Reading the newspapers as you do, you would have known that commodities prices were on a strong upward trend, due to a number of factors including increased global demand, harvest shortfalls, and mandates for ethanol production. Moreover, commodities are U.S. dollar denominated, and the dollar was losing value. When the dollar slides versus other currencies, commodities become more expensive. You also would have known that if commodities prices increase, the last place you want to be invested is in packaged-foods manufacturers. The cost of raw materials would be heading higher for packaged-foods manufacturers. Whereas, they might be able to pass some of those costs on to the consumer, mostly higher costs would simply erode their profit margins. There is only so much that a consumer would be willing to pay for a bowl of cereal.

In 2007, if you wanted to gain access to the Industrial Goods sector, Deere proved clearly to be a better choice, both from a historical perspective (by the genius of hindsight) and looking forward (by an informed forecast of industry dynamics) relative to ConAgra. You would not have had to crunch a single number to figure that out.

The national and international newspapers at the time were crowing every day about the trend opportunity: global demand was forcing commodities prices up. ConAgra made a bunch of money trading commodities, but market investors rewarded the fundamental play that Deere offered instead. There was great reason: increases in commodities prices lead to an increase in "planted" agricultural acreages of agribusiness. That in turn lead to greater purchases of plants and equipment, which would benefit companies in the Farm and Construction Machinery industry, such as Deere. On the other hand, higher commodities prices did not represent an opportunity for Packaged Goods companies. Higher commodities prices meant higher costs, only some of which could be passed through to the consumer. An erosion of profit margins was inevitable. Long Farm Equipment, short Packaged Goods (finished product) was the play under these macroeconomic conditions.

The starkly different price performances of these two companies in the face of increasing commodities prices was reflected in their respective price advances. Deere far outperformed ConAgra. The cost of such outperformance was some additional volatility, i.e., the variability in Deere's price from month to month. It is evident in the graph that Deere is more volatile than ConAgra. The variance from point to point is higher, so Deere could be viewed as a riskier asset. But you can clearly see in the graph that the extra volatility in Deere is more than compensated for by its superior return relative to ConAgra's.

In retrospect, it would be obvious to say that these two stocks would have made a great hedge as a pairs trade. If you were long Deere and short ConAgra, from the beginning of 2007, it would have indeed been a sweet trade. Hindsight is benefiting us here, but in real time, there could and should have been a point at which it would have made sense as a hedge position. Any investor must be careful about looking back and projecting forward, a potential pitfall known as data mining. Be careful, because once you have been "convinced" that an observed opportunity may be profitable, the opportunity may already be gone. If you have observed it, you could already be late to the game. Most trend followers attempt to capture 60 percent of a trend, then exit. Be careful not to come to the profit party too late—it could be closing down.

Earlier in my career, I ran quantitative investment strategies. Raising capital was a tough sell because precious few investors believed in quantitative techniques and statistical analysis. One potential investor seethed at me after my quantitative presentation of betas, alphas, correlation coefficients, and Sharpe Ratios. "[This] company would *never* invest in a strategy that depended on historical patterns to make viable forecasts!" Then he angrily kicked me out of his office for the temerity of my suggestions. I took it on the chin and set about doing exactly what he claimed could not be done. You see, every strategy known to man uses historical information to make forecasts. *Every* strategy other than random selection uses historical knowledge to make informed projections. When you invest, you bet that a trend will either continue or reverse. You will be long, short, or flat. No matter what detailed fundamental analysis I do, I always seek to confirm or dispel the idea with a graph. You should too. You would be surprised how it could change your mind or refine your conviction on a trade.

The market concurred with me on the hedge of Deere and ConAgra, and it piled in on the trade and showed its conviction with share volume. At the bottom of the price chart is the daily volume of equity shares sold in these companies. Volume is another valuable data item for those who wish to avoid the fundamental number crunch. Notice that every time Deere had a "breakout" versus ConAgra, the trading volume also kicked up. During high-volume periods, Deere increased the spread of its performance relative to ConAgra's. That's an important observation because it means that when investors were paying attention to the sector, and to these stocks in particular, they confirmed the validity of the hedge between the two with share volume. At lower share volumes, the market's sentiment was less clear, because fewer investors were trading. Price movement during low volume is tantamount to noise.

When there was definitive price movement at high volume, however, the market clearly prefers Deere over ConAgra. Look for volume as another indicator of the market's sentiment for your ideas.

Let us introduce another element to the graph: the performance of the broad market index, the S&P 500.

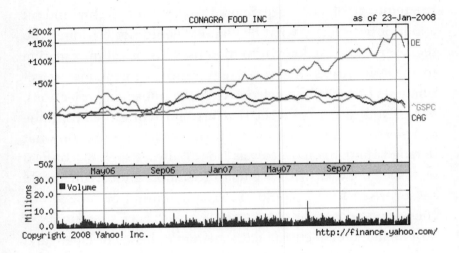

The performance of any security relative to the broad market, the S&P 500, tells you a lot. In the graph above, we added the time series of GSPC the symbol for the S&P 500 Index. The S&P 500 is the widely accepted benchmark for broad market performance. The S&P 500 price series demonstrates that *ConAgra's price performance did not outperform the market.* We know from earlier chapters that, in accordance with Modern Portfolio Theory, individual stock movements are 85 percent driven by the market. The 15 percent balance is driven by idiosyncratic advantages or weaknesses individually inherent to each company. ConAgra's price performance achieved what analysts call Market Perform, meaning that there is nothing exceptional about the company versus its peers: its performance mirrors that of the market overall. ConAgra did not perform better or worse than the average company in the S&P 500. Compared to the rest of the market, ConAgra gets a C. Deere, on the other hand, significantly outperformed ConAgra and the market overall, so it gets an A+.

The outperformance of an individual security or an asset or an investment or a portfolio over broad market performance is known as alpha, the elusive target for every hedge manager. It is also called the excess return to the market, adjusting for risk. The alpha metric recognizes the difference between a very risky stock that outperforms the market and a less risky stock that outperforms the market, stably and consistently. Risky stocks could underperform the market significantly the very next measurement period. We can conclude that in its sector, Deere is a superior performer both relative to its peers and relative to the market. Without crunching a single number, we have made a conclusion that is the foundation for a profitable hedge.

It would be imprudent to completely abandon hard data. It is true that a graph can say a lot, but technical analysis (the science of interpreting graphs and making forecasts) has its limitations. Remember, every other investor is armed with data tools and tracks the Fave Five closely (and probably other indicators as well). You need to, too.

Balance Sheets, Income Statements, and Financial Ratios

There is a mountain of actionable data contained in annual reports, including balance sheets and income statements. Interpreting these statements is both science and art. Learning to parse them for hidden value or risk is what makes the great investors great. We will not analyze financial statements extensively here. There are volumes of texts that have useful (and extensive) explanations. *Investments*, by William Sharpe, is a great reference tool, for example. But I stick to our mantra that if you have a little information and trust your instincts, you will be able to analyze these statements to your advantage. You need to know the very basics.

When you look at fundamental data contained in the financial statements of a company, note that the numbers are not as relevant standalone as they are relative to the values of peers. The price/earnings ratio of a company means more to the investor when compared to that of peer companies than as an absolute number. Even more important is the *history and trend* of a particular financial ratio over time historically. A static ratio is a single photo that says a thousand words, but a historical time series of the same ratios is a financial movie that brings data to life. It will enhance your investment decision-making. When regarding the financial ratios, you should concentrate on how these data have changed over time historically and try to project how they will change going forward. Charting a graph of the changes in fundamental data is a way of watching the movie.

Rated fundamental data are also quite useful. Rated data in financial statements are the data represented by a ratio of one fundamental item to another. The financial ratios are the foundation for analyzing a company and its attractiveness relative to other potential investments. A fundamental ratio normalizes the items for comparison and it is what makes a static, fundamental item relevant. For example, 186,000 miles is a long way but is otherwise unremarkable. The relevance of 186,000 miles is significantly enhanced when it is expressed as a ratio, such as 186,000 miles per second, or the speed of light.

Price becomes significant when divided by earnings. A stock price, say $43 per share, really cannot say much about a company. You would not even have an idea of a company's total value unless you also knew the total number of shares outstanding, say 121 million shares. The total value of the company is then $5.2 billion. Now you *know* something! Similarly, a price of $43 does not tell you what the market thinks about this company's prospects relative to its peers—unless you know the *earnings* per share, $2.80. Divide the price by the earnings, and a 15 P/E ratio suggests that the market is willing to pay for the shares to an imputed return on equity of 7 percent (earnings/price). What is the price/earnings ratio of similar companies? Ask yourself why.

The next place to look is the competitors' financial ratios. Is the market evaluating this company consistently with the sector? With the industry? The comparison of target companies is called "comps" or "comparables." Comps are very useful in determining relative value and therefore potential hedges in your portfolio. When looking at the rated data (one fundamental item divided by another) for a stock, take a look at how it compares to that of other stocks in the sector or industry. For example, the PEG ratio of two solid companies in the same sector may suggest that you invest in one (the lower PEG) instead of the other (higher PEG). The thinking is that the company with the higher PEG may have reached its peak relative to its future growth. Its lower PEG "friend" might be a better value.

Below are the typical summary financial data presented on Yahoo! Finance for each traded security. I think the online sites do a fine job of parsing out the critical elements from the balance sheets and income statements of publicly traded companies. To bring some meaning to these data, I asked a friend to arbitrarily choose a stock and provide me with the financial data only, so that I could render a blind, quick and dirty assessment. Take a look at each item and form your own opinion.

Key Statistics

VALUATION MEASURES

Market Cap: 145.28B
Huge company, not going anywhere south—
probably

Enterprise Value: 167.73B
EV is an alternative valuation[6]

Trailing P/E (ttm): 14.55
P/E is below or near the historical average for
the market = good value

Forward P/E: 11.35
Growth expectations are sound

PEG Ratio
(5 yr expected): 1.21
My favorite. Significantly less than the market's
1.8

Price/Sales (ttm): 1.50
Not a strong ratio b/c it does not take operations into consideration

Price/Book (mrq): 5.22
Book value is breakup value. The higher P/B
is your "equity" at risk

Enterprise Value/
Revenue (ttm): 1.70
No comment, same as price/sales

Enterprise Value/
EBITDA (ttm): 8.546
Similar to P/E. Tells you your cash return is
1/8.5 = 12 percent. Not bad.

---

6. EV is calculated as market cap plus debt, minority interest, and preferred
shares, minus total cash and cash equivalents.

FINANCIAL HIGHLIGHTS

Fiscal Year

Fiscal Year Ends: 31–Dec

Most Recent Quarter (mrq): 31–Dec-07

Profitability

Profit Margin (ttm): 10.55%

Profit margins vary by industry, but 11 percent is strong

Operating Margin
(ttm): 14.65%

Also strong. Operating margins are before expenses not directly due to operations

Management Effectiveness

Return on Assets
(ttm): 8.09%

Compared to the statistic below, suggests it is an asset-intensive business. Fairly low but okay.

Return on Equity
(ttm): 36.57%

Nice!

Income Statement

Revenue (ttm): 98.79B

Suggests size by market capitalization, itself a "style factor"

Revenue Per Share
(ttm): 69.422

ditto

Qtrly Revenue
Growth (yoy): 9.90%

Ten percent growth year over year suggests a growth company

Gross Profit (ttm):   38.30B

EBITDA (ttm):   19.63B

Net Income Avl to
Common (ttm):   10.42B

This is 10B in your pocket every year if you are the owner. How much would you pay for that? Measure that answer against the P/E.

Diluted EPS (ttm):   7.18

Qtrly Earnings
Growth (yoy):   11.60%

Earnings growth is higher than revenue growth. Suggests increasing efficiencies or cost cutting

Balance Sheet

Total Cash (mrq):   16.15B

Sure can do a lot with that 16B of cash on hand. Acquisition, anyone?

Total Cash Per
Share (mrq):   11.616

Total Debt (mrq):   35.27B

Total Debt/Equity
(mrq):   1.239

Not debt laden

Current Ratio
(mrq):   1.112

ditto

Book Value Per
Share (mrq):   20.482

Cash Flow Statement

Operating Cash
Flow (ttm):   N/A

Levered Free Cash
Flow (ttm):   N/A

TRADING INFORMATION

Stock Price History

Beta: 1.59

Beta is an overused metric, but it suggests that this company is highly sensitive to the performance of the market overall.

52–Week Change: 7.26%

Nonetheless, the company has significantly outperformed the market when the market is in the red. That suggests resilience and noncorrelated return. Good stuff.

S&P500 52–Week
Change: -6.44%

The market showed a nearly inverse performance relative to this company. The company had an alpha of almost 13 percent.

52–Week High: 121.46

52–Week Low: 88.77

50–Day Moving
Average: 105.30

200–Day Moving
Average: 110.80

Share Statistics

Average Volume
(3 month):   9,198,750

Average Volume
(10 day):   14,735,700

The recent market period has seen a serious spike in share-volume trading activity. I would compare this increase to the market volume increase. If the increase in this company is disproportionately higher, it suggests that the market sees an actionable item in this company or sector.

Shares
Outstanding: 1.39B

Float: 1.39B

% Held by
Insiders: 0.05%

% Held by
Institutions: 63.30%

Shares Short
(as of 26–Dec-07):   17.66M

Short Ratio
(as of 26–Dec-07):   2.5

Short % of Float
(as of 26–Dec-07):   1.30%

> One of the lowest short percentages of total float you will ever see. The market does not bet against this company because it is a proven performer.

Shares Short
(prior month):   14.67M

Dividends & Splits

Forward Annual
Dividend Rate: 1.60

Forward Annual
Dividend Yield: 1.50%

Trailing Annual
Dividend Rate: 1.50

Trailing Annual
Dividend Yield: 1.40%

5 Year Average
Dividend Yield: 0.80%

Payout Ratio: 21%

> Twenty-one percent of earnings are paid out to you in cash, which is strong. This could

be an income company. The rest of earnings
is plowed back into the company to fuel
company growth and capital appreciation.
This has the hallmarks of a mature growth
company.

Dividend Date:	10–Dec-07
Ex-Dividend Date:	07–Nov-07
Last Split Factor (new per old):	2:1

After this sixty-second speed exercise, my friend told me
that the company represented by the financial data above is
IBM. So I was not far off with my assessment that it was a stable
growth company. Some quantitative analysis—even cursory—
can be powerful to identify attractive relative performers in a
given industry or sector. I encourage you strongly to consider
these data—they are *free*—on every company before you take a
position long or short. Over time, you will surprise yourself at
your skill in identifying targets. Such practice will also prevent
you from impulsively buying the next hot idea or stock that has
no chance of survival; many of the fundamental data would
show warning signs, like a deteriorating margin or declining
year-to-year growth. Finally, look at historical values for your
favorite ratios. They will give you a sound sense of the direction
the company in which you're interested is going.

ETFs

I love Exchange Traded Funds (ETFs). They are one of
the most effective instruments available to you to effect
hedge strategies in your own portfolio. With ETFs, you can
truly accomplish what the professionals do. ETFs offer an
elegant way to avoid the drudgery of determining the security level analysis. The work is already done for you. You

can express any macro view with an ETF, just like hedge fund managers do.

Before the availability of ETFs, it was more difficult to invest in market themes. ETFs are preformed baskets of securities that trade collectively as a portfolio, available as a single security, on the stock exchanges. They are specifically priced to accommodate the smaller trade sizes of the average investor. You can long or short ETFs, focusing on specific areas of investment opportunities with a large and ever-growing menu of industries, styles, and themes.

In 2007, I was long a portfolio of a few energy stocks that really worked well for me. I had done my research, compared the financial ratios, and compiled a group of stocks I felt would reflect my view that the energy sector would significantly outperform the S&P 500. I thought I was clever. But take a look at the constituents of one of the best known energy ETFs, the Energy Select Sector SPDR (XLE), below. The ETF was holding many of the same stocks I was holding. A small investor who didn't know jack about individual company analysis could have assembled a portfolio of energy stocks that looked just like mine (or better) simply by buying the Energy Select ETF. The ETF has only twenty or so stocks in the entire portfolio. It is focused on the key energy stocks, with only ten positions representing 66 percent of the ETF's value.

Holdings: As of 30–Nov-07

Top 10 Holdings (66.39% of Total Assets)

APACHE CP *APA*	2.68
CHEVRON CORP *CVX*	12.52

CONOCOPHILLIPS	
COP	8.85
DEVON ENERGY CP (OK)	
DVN	2.91
EXXON MOBIL CP	
XOM	20.57
MARATHON OIL CORP	
MRO	3.16
OCCIDENTAL PET	
OXY	4.3
SCHLUMBERGER LTD	
SLB	5.16
TRANSOCEAN INC	
RIG	3.47
VALERO ENERGY CP	
VLO	2.77

I had spent a good deal of time trying to figure out the portfolio that would express my views on the Energy sector, but I could have accomplished the same outcome by buying the ETF, a benchmark for the sector. The Energy sector ETF had weightings for each stock that were slightly different from the weightings I put together in my portfolio. On the whole, though, the performance was the same. Moreover, the ETF included some ideas and securities that I had not even thought of. Why? Because that was the ETF manager's sole focus. *Buying an ETF is like having the world's greatest experts on hand to devise a way for you to act on whatever financial idea comes to mind.*

Remember the Agribusiness companies we discussed earlier? We chose Deere because we sought to benefit from the increase in farmed acreage as commodity prices rose. Well, there was an ETF that focused on the same opportunity—

MarketVectors ETF (MOO), which is based on the DAX-global Agribusiness Index (DXAG). For my portfolio, I was impressed with Deere's performance as a stand-alone way to express my view on commodities and their impact on agri-business equipment manufacturers. I selected one stock to express my view, Deere, whereas the MOO ETF expressed the same idea with multiple stocks. This ETF is *always* tilted to the Agribusiness sector. The top seven stocks represent more than 50 percent of the ETF. If you wanted to play the agri-business idea, long or short, this ETF already had the necessary exposures and positions. All you had to do was buy the ETF or sell it, depending upon your view.

Below is a chart of the performance of the top stocks in the ETF.

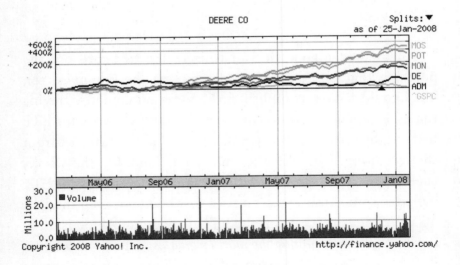

Top 10 Holdings (64.82% of Total Assets)

BUNGE LTD		
BG	4.36	
CNH GLOBAL NV		
CNH	4.48	
DEERE CO		
DE	7.28	
IOI		
N/A	5.08	
KOMATSU LTD		
N/A	7.33	
MONSANTO COMPANY		
MON	8.57	
POTASH CP SASKATCHEW		
POT	8.24	
MOSAIC COMPANY (THE)		
MOS	9.56	
WILMAR		
F34.SI	4.73	
YARA INTERNATIONAL		
YAR.OL	5.19	

The MOO ETF did a great job of capturing the same phenomenon I had achieved by purchasing Deere. Since some of the companies MOO invested in were international, it reaped the further benefit of a currency profit, too.

In fact, the ETF *beat* me and my picks for the sector. MOO's top five holdings averaged 292 percent, far in excess of the 110 percent return I earned with the Deere/ConAgra long/short trade. I am not crying, but I was impressed with the ETF. And the overall risk of the ETF portfolio was substantially lower relative to a stand-alone Deere position. Last, buying the ETF obviates the need to analyze each company for the fundamentals. It saves time. The result was an ETF with a supercompetitive, well-constructed portfolio with less risk than my single-security trade.

The ETF also benefited from scale economies. If you had wanted to assemble the same basket of securities that are held in the ETF, you would have had to spend at least $35,000, assuming hundred-share minimum lots for each company. Yet the ETF was available to you for as little as $100. The small investor is thus significantly empowered. For $100, you could achieve the same exposures and portfolio companies as a hedge fund manager. And the profit of $400 would have been just as sweet. I did well with Deere/ConAgra, but the ETF kicked my tail. I have begun to use ETFs more often.

Odd as it sounds, the objective of most ETFs is not superior performance to the sector benchmarks, per se. The objective of most ETFs is to achieve the same performance as their benchmarks precisely. If a particular sector is out of favor, then its ETF will precisely yield out-of-favor returns (which would be profitable if you were short the ETF). An S&P 500 ETF, for example, will not seek to outperform the S&P 500; its objective is to give the same return as the S & P 500. If the S&P 500 return is down, so too will be the ETF.

But there is comfort in that dependability. There is no style drift. You buy the ETF and know precisely what you are going to get. If you have "hired" a manager through an ETF purchase to get long-term exposure to utilities, you do not want the manager switching to Brazilian alternative energy IPOs to make more money. You want just the opposite. You want the manager to precisely represent the sector you purchased—for better or worse—so you know exactly what you are getting. The ETF performance and portfolio selection should be exactly as advertised.

Knowing which sector to transact in and having an idea of how much of your assets to allocate is key, but once done, the ETF will do the rest. Some of the ETFs in favor and out of favor for 2007 are listed below. The worst-performing ETFs were down more than 50 percent for the year; the winners exceeded a 50 percent return. The winning themes included Energy, Metals, and the emerging markets of Asia and Latin America. The losing themes for the year included, predictably for 2007, Financials and Real Estate. As you peruse the winners and losers, note that the winners all fit into themes we could have picked up with our Fave Fives and by reading the ordinary news headlines.

Fund Name	Ticker	Category	Fund Family	12Mos.
iPath MSCI India Index ETN	INP	Pacific/Asia ex-Japan Stk	Barclays Bank PLC	86.44%
Market Vectors Steel ETF	SLX	Specialty-Natural Res	Market Vectors Etf Trust	84.35%
iShares MSCI Brazil Index	EWZ	Latin America Stock	iShares, Inc.	74.83%
Claymore/BNY BRIC	EEB	Diversified Emerging Mkts	Claymore Exchange-traded Fund Trust	67.30%
PowerShares Gldn DragonUSX China	PGJ	Pacific/Asia ex-Japan Stk	PowerShares Exchange Traded Fund Trust	63.27%
PowerShares WilderHill Clean Engy	PBW	Specialty-Natural Res	PowerShares Exchange Traded Fund Trust	58.50%
iShares FTSE/Xinhua China 25	FXI	Pacific/Asia ex-Japan Stk	iShares Trust	54.75%
iShares S&P Lat Am 40	ILF	Latin America Stock	iShares Trust	48.48%
GSCI Crude Oil Tot Ret Idx	OIL	Specialty-Natural Res	Barclays Bank PLC	47.53%
United States Oil	USO	Specialty-Natural Res	United States Oil Fund, LP	46.82%
MACROshares Oil Up Shares	UCR	Specialty-Natural Res	Macro Securities Depositor, LLC	44.88%
iShares MSCI Malaysia Index	EWM	Pacific/Asia ex-Japan Stk	iShares, Inc.	44.59%
BLDRS Emg Mkts 50 ADR Index	ADRE	Diversified Emerging Mkts	BLDRS Index Funds Trust	43.89%
iShares US Oil Equipment Index	IEZ	Specialty-Natural Res	iShares Funds	42.64%
PowerShares Cleantech	PZD	Small Growth	PowerShares Exchange Traded Fund Trust	41.95%
SPDR S&P Metals & Mining	XME	Specialty-Natural Res	Spdr Series Trust	41.74%
Rydex S&P Equal Weight Energy	RYE	Specialty-Natural Res	Rydex ETF Trust	40.18%
iShares US Oil & Gas Ex Index	IEO	Specialty-Natural Res	iShares Funds	39.62%
iShares MSCI Hong Kong Index	EWH	Pacific/Asia ex-Japan Stk	iShares, Inc.	39.42%
PowerShares Oil & Gas Svcs	PXJ	Specialty-Natural Res	PowerShares Exchange Traded Fund Trust	39.34%
Rydex S&P Eql Wt Financials	RYF	Specialty-Financial	Rydex ETF Trust	-17.38%
Vanguard Financials	VFH	Specialty-Financial	Vanguard Index Funds	-17.58%
iShares US Financial Sector	IYF	Specialty-Financial	iShares Trust	-18.05%
iShares US Real Estate	IYR	Specialty-Real Estate	iShares Trust	-18.11%
PowerShares FTSE RAFI Financials	PRFF	Specialty-Financial	PowerShares Exchange Traded Fund Trust	-18.17%
DJ Wilshire REIT ETF	RWR	Specialty-Real Estate	Spdr Series Trust	-18.20%
iShares CohenSteers Realty Majors	ICF	Specialty-Real Estate	iShares Trust	-18.21%
Regional Bank HOLDRs	RKH	Specialty-Financial	Merrill Lynch, Pierce, Fenner & Smith	-18.63%
Rydex S&P Smallcap 600 Pure Value	RZV	Small Value	Rydex ETF Trust	-19.06%
PowerShares Dynamic Retail	PMR	Large Blend	PowerShares Exchange Traded Fund Trust	-19.14%
Financial Select SPDR	XLF	Specialty-Financial	Select Sector Spdr Trust	-19.19%
KBW Bank ETF	KBE	Specialty-Financial	Spdr Series Trust	-21.68%
iShares US Financial Services	IYG	Specialty-Financial	iShares Trust	-21.84%
PowerShares Dynamic Banking	PJB	Specialty-Financial	PowerShares Exchange Traded Fund Trust	-21.87%
KBW Regional Banking ETF	KRE	Specialty-Financial	Spdr Series Trust	-23.15%
iShares US Regional Banks	IAT	Specialty-Financial	iShares Funds	-25.48%
UltraShort QQQ ProShares	QID	Bear Market	ProShares Trust	-27.36%
MACROshares Oil Down	DCR	Specialty-Natural Res	Macro Securities Depositor, LLC	-45.29%
SPDR S&P Homebuilders	XHB	Mid-Cap Value	Spdr Series Trust	-47.66%
iShares US Home Construction	ITB	Large Blend	iShares Funds	-57.87%

In 2007, the spread return between the top twenty and the bottom twenty ETFs was 160 percent. This means that if you had gotten your hedge sectors right, there was a profitable reward from being long/short in ETFs. Does the Fave Five have you thinking that utilities are going down? Short the utilities ETF. Want to short the Dow? Buy DXDs. Want to get exposure to agribusiness worldwide or energy companies? Buy the MarketVectors agribusiness or energy funds, respectively. Think gold is going to increase? There is an ETF for that. You think energy-related stocks are going to take off? There is an ETF you can buy whose top-ten holdings are the ten most relevant energy stocks available. Instead of having to buy ten securities, you can buy one laser-focused ETF.

Since ETFs first became available, they have significantly expanded their product offerings. They put genius at the fingertips of the average investor. The ETFs allow the investor to get immediate and quick sector or strategic exposure, like a big hedge manager calling his trading desk and exercising futures. If you are effecting top-down (sector-based) conclusions about which directions and exposures you would like to take with respect to the market, ETFs will serve you well.

Constructing a hedge fund strategy is not as abstruse as it appears. The major themes can be easily detected, as we have discussed. And through ETFs you can sidestep some of the company-level data analyses necessary to construct a portfolio. The ETFs do it for you. Get the themes right long *and* short, and you have really conquered the market.

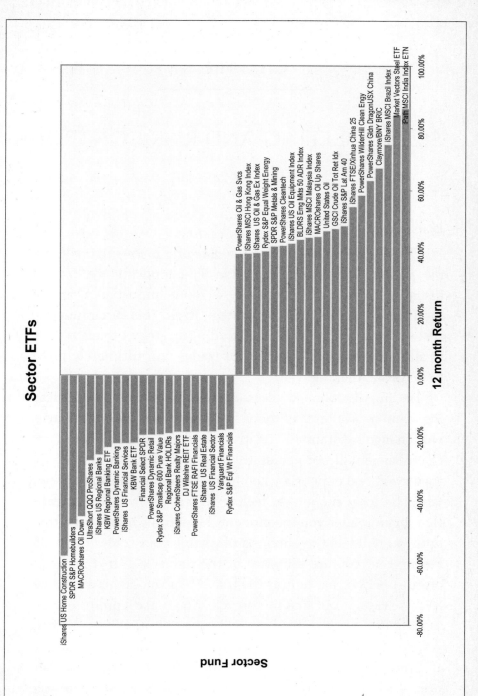

Sector ETFs

Sector Fund

12 month Return

iShares US Home Construction
SPDR S&P Homebuilders
MACROshares Oil Down
UltraShort QQQ ProShares
iShares US Regional Banks
KBW Regional Banking ETF
PowerShares Dynamic Banking
iShares US Financial Services
KBW Bank ETF
Financial Select SPDR
PowerShares Dynamic Retail
Rydex S&P Smallcap 600 Pure Value
Regional Bank HOLDRs
iShares CohenSteers Realty Majors
DJ Wilshire REIT ETF
PowerShares FTSE RAFI Financials
iShares US Real Estate
iShares US Financial Sector
Vanguard Financials
Rydex S&P Eql Wt Financials

PowerShares Oil & Gas Svcs
iShares MSCI Hong Kong Index
iShares US Oil & Gas Ex Index
Rydex S&P Equal Weight Energy
SPDR S&P Metals & Mining
PowerShares Cleantech
iShares US Oil Equipment Index
BLDRS Emg Mkts 50 ADR Index
iShares MSCI Malaysia Index
MACROshares Oil Up Shares
United States Oil
GSCI Crude Oil Tot Ret Idx
iShares S&P Lat Am 40
iShares FTSE/Xinhua China 25
PowerShares WilderHill Clean Engy
PowerShares Gldn DragonUSX China
Claymore/BNY BRIC
iShares MSCI Brazil Index
Market Vectors Steel ETF
iPath MSCI India Index ETN

-80.00% -60.00% -40.00% -20.00% 0.00% 20.00% 40.00% 60.00% 80.00% 100.00%

CHAPTER 8

SIZING, SELLING, AND RISK CONTROL

Discipline

The single most important attribute of a successful investor is the quality of his trading discipline. The application of trading discipline to a trading strategy is more important than the intelligence underlying the strategy itself. It is discipline that sustains a great trader and his trading strategy because statistically only about 50 percent of trades will ultimately prove to be profit-making.

Trading discipline is necessary because success is intoxicating—and so is failure. Without discipline, your trading behavior will change substantially relative to yours wins and losses and that change will not necessarily be productive. Inevitably, the trader will feel euphoria when he makes money and depression when he loses money—a feeling so strong, from experience, that it can render you incontinent. Hopefully, more often than not, you will feel the euphoria of getting your trades right, the feeling that you are a master of the universe. Yet it is just as often euphoria that tempts the trader to abandon his discipline. It is like riding your first motorcycle. You make a promise yourself to obey every traffic light and speed limit. Within a week, you are doing wheelies, craving speed, and splitting lanes.

Emotional trading is a slow-cook recipe for long-term failure. With trading discipline, you should achieve measured results and, over the long term, perform well, or at least consistently. Trading is littered with roadkill. For every trader you read about who is sipping Cristal from the deck of his yacht, there are thousands of traders with a decidedly less compelling outcome—a sob story. Honestly, I cannot count how many New York cabdrivers let me know that "Yeah, I used to trade for [Morgan Stanley] [Lehman Brothers] [Merrill Lynch] [Goldman Sachs] [JPMorganChase] [NYMEX], etc." It would seem that Wall Street is a prep course for becoming a gharry-wallah. The markets are challenging, and having a system of discipline gives you a leg up on your trading. The practice that advances and sustains the successful trader is developing and adhering to his trading discipline.

Admittedly, I have always favored quantitative, or rule-based, trading systems. At the end of the day, every trading strategy is a study of human behavior. Systems remove the emotional component. Systems do not get tired, they rarely experience hubris, they do not have arguments with their significant others, and they are not proud. They do require thoughtful calibration and periodic tweaking, because no matter how well a system is designed, markets change. Regime shifts occur, and systems must adjust with them. That is the advantage the discretionary trader has over quant strategies: the human mind is the greatest computer there is and it can adjust faster and more logically than most systems when markets change.

I recognize that trade discipline is boring. To be one's own risk manager is contrary to all things fun about being a trader. The idea of a trade discipline, however, is not to avoid risk but to take risks intelligently. It is inevitable that exercising discipline will leave profits on the table from time to time. Undoubtedly there will be times when you could have made more profit from a particular trade if you had abandoned your discipline. But it is better to hit singles and doubles and quit than to push it and take on a reward/risk ratio that has diminished. The magnitudes of wins and losses in the typical portfolio are proportional, i.e., normally distributed. It is the discipline of knowing when to close a position that skews those wins and losses into a winning strategy.

Andrew Weisman, CIO of Merrill Lynch's Alternative Trading Group, puts it another way. He calls it Andy's Law:

Andy's Law 1: In any trading strategy, over the long run, the magnitude of losses will be proportional to the magnitude of wins.

Andy's Law 2: The magnitude of the losses experienced by a strategy is inversely proportional to the probability of their occurrence.

Law 1 is an obvious result; the more a trader seeks to win, the more he is in a position to lose, because to seek greater gain, he necessarily must take on greater risk. Experienced hedge fund investors are keenly aware that outsized positive returns are a clear indicator of the possibility of outsized loss potential.

Law 2 is a somewhat less obvious yet more important trading phenomenon in terms of risk potential. Andy's Law 2 implies that the less frequent a manager's losses, the longer a trader goes without a loss, the greater the loss will be once it does come. This is not written in stone, of course, but follows empirical observations that Andy has made during his extensive study of hedge fund managers. Certain classes of managers tend to produce virtually flawless performance histories, right up until their meltdowns. The most renowned example of this law expressing itself in the real world is of course Long Term Capital, which was a model of consistency until the end came and the fund collapsed from irrevocable losses. Similarly, the best market neutral funds, supposedly impervious to losses, had lost as much as 30 percent in 2007, after years of consistently positive returns. And trend followers certainly show this dynamic—five great years up then one big one down—which we have discussed before.

I do not mean to suggest that there is a magic discipline that works in all cases or for all traders. Nor is it to suggest that once you have developed an investment discipline you like, it should stay the same. Any systematic discipline will evolve over time, as will the characteristics of the markets or companies in which you will trade. Rules are important, but they must evolve. It is imperative that you be vigilant with respect to your discipline but not immutable.

Any trade discipline would be meaningless if it were not specifically suited to your risk tolerance, risk preferences, personality, and performance targets. But I can tell you this—*every* successful hedge manager has his own discipline. The good ones are sustainable over time. Each trader's discipline is as unique as his own personality. Each trader has a different appetite for risk and has a different goal for performance. Traders in the same space can have vastly different disciplines, yet still be profitable. The best advice regarding a discipline is that *you should have one*. It could be as simple as "I leave a trade on as long as the unrealized gain is between –1 percent and 8 percent or twenty trading days—whichever is sooner." That could be a perfectly valid trading system for minimizing the variability of your returns. And if you are making good picks, such a simple strategy would likely make money over time.

As your trading evolves, you might step up the sophistication: "My trading strategy is a decision tree based on these rules: 1) I leave a trade on as long as the realizable profit is between –1 percent and 8 percent or a maximum of twenty trading days; 2) Once a trade breaks a threshold of 8 percent I sell short-dated at-the-money call options against it to enhance my profit or, alternatively, 2a) I buy successive put options against it to insure my profit."

I am making these up (although they aren't bad). The rules of your discipline should be specific to your personal objectives. For example, when I go to Vegas, I love to play craps. I became a fan of craps because the first time I visited a casino, in my teens, knowing nothing and living near enough to Atlantic City, I bought a book describing all of the games of chance in the casino. I studied the games and determined that craps had the best odds for the player (if played correctly) and was the most fun. That was a winning proposition for me.

In craps, the player can either maximize his time at the table or maximize the magnitude of the payouts. When I want to maximize my time at the table, I play 6 and 8 straight because together, they represent the highest probability for the occurrence of a payout—a probability of 10 in 36 versus crapping out with 7, which is 6 in 36. Playing those odds should win me steady money in nominal amounts. Once I have built up some "house money" and I want the best probability of winning big bucks, I take double odds on the marks and always play the Come. The former strategy can last for hours, while the latter maximizes payout but leaves a lot of money at risk.

The point is that a disciplined strategy for placing bets ensured that I never lost my shirt, my losses were limited, and the upside was limitless. Which craps strategy I choose will depend on my appetite for risk. That's sort of what we want out of a good trade.

Back-Testing

There are programs available that allow investors to back-test their investment discipline. MetaStock and programs like it can test your trading philosophies on historical market periods and tell you whether they would have been profitable. Fidelity and other retail brokerages now provide a free trading platform that accomplishes the same thing. It is a useful exercise, but be wary of overemphasizing the conclusions. Back-testing can be a valuable tool for pointing you in the right direction, but you could also end up employing strategies that would have worked well in the past but have no hopes of working well in the future (as per Andy's Law 2). A strategy, for example, that tested well in December 1999 may have been to mortgage everything you own to buy Internet technology stocks. But it would have been a disaster in March 2000. In all the years I have evaluated the trading systems of potential hires, I have never seen a back-test by a would-be trader that was not wildly successful. More often than not the real-time application of the back-tested strategy yielded less-than-stellar results.

Know your objectives clearly, and devise a discipline that works for you.

Sizing Your Trades

One of my responsibilities over the years has been to interview candidates for trading positions. In the early years, I was concerned with seeming tough and difficult to convince. I had a mean disposition. With more experience, I learned to listen; I wanted to hear a prospective trader's insights. Assessing a trader's investment philosophies is like reading a novel: some are trashy, others pedantic, but in the end, they all have a moral. (By the way, if you ever interview for a trader position, know that the interviewers—intentionally or not—will cherry-pick your good ideas. It is inescapable.)

What was commonly the case, especially for those traders who were purely discretionary, is that I would hear great ideas, sometimes brilliant ones, but the trader rarely had a clue about how much of the portfolio should be allocated to a particular trade. I would say, "Great idea. How would you determine how much of your money you would put into this trade, or any trade? Tell me the impact your trade would have on the whole portfolio performance? Do you know? If a trade goes against you, what do you do? Do you double down or cut and run? Do you take concentrated positions, i.e., allocate large portions of your capital to a particular trade? Do you have position limits or risk ceilings or loss thresholds?

Sizing your trades will depend on how you answer the following questions: 1. What is the desired contribution of this position to the overall risk of the portfolio? 2. How much risk (loss) am I willing to tolerate? You need to know these answers *before* you enter any position. These are your guidelines.

There is no singular answer because answers will vary with the market conditions and investment target. There are a few guidelines, however, you can use that will benefit your overall performance. Without them, your first lessons about risk control could be a brutal surprise. In trading parlance, a "lesson" usually arises from a negative experience, a loss.

I once worked with a hard-charging trader. He was brash, loud, and quick-tempered. He could be seen at all times of the trading day with multiple phones stuck to his head. He was singularly, if not pathologically, devoted to his trading screens, but his trading acumen did not match his desire to succeed. He was a true riskophile, tending to bet on concentrated positions so that his p&l fluctuated with the fortunes of just a few positions. His lack of attention to controlling risk made him a nervous wreck, suffering from the advances and declines of his "overweight" positions.

After spending years at the investment banks, Karim, we

shall call him, decided to start his own hedge fund. One day, I asked him how he had earned the capital to start his own fund. His story began with being fired from a major investment bank six months into a two-year contract. Karim was eager to show his former employers what a mistake they had made by letting him go.

He had been the head of the overnight repurchase ("repo") desk—arguably the easiest trading assignment on the Street. The investment bank's repo trading program was sufficiently routine, so there was hardly any room to muss it up. It was like being the Maytag repairman; the product takes care of itself. No one gets fired from such an assignment but Karim had a difficult personality, to put it mildly. The bank preferred to pay him the rest of his contract, $1 million, in upfront cash rather than endure his tenure for twelve more months.

Karim took the money and immediately set about trading for himself. "I will show them," he thought. Using his contacts, he was able to get set up quickly with the trading accounts and the credit lines necessary to trade. His very first trade was in Japanese Government Bonds (JGBs). At that time, everyone was shorting JGBs because of the carry trade, a common hedge strategy in fixed income instruments. By shorting JGBs, one would take in cash like any other short, and invest in a higher-yielding sovereign debt, like U.S. Treasury bonds, and pocket the spread. The cost of the trade is to pay the interest on the short bond. The carry trade, with the right pairs, is tantamount to a free annuity, as long as bond prices remain stable.

My friend Karim wanted to get about $5 million of short exposure not in a hedge but as a directional play. That might not seem possible if you have only $1 million in the bank, but since bond prices are relatively stable, the brokerage houses only require investors to put up a small fraction of the face value of the transaction, which provides leverage to the desired bet. In order for Karim to get $5 million of JGBs, he would only need to provide collateral of, say, $250,000. That was a small enough portion of his overall capital that he would not have to worry too much if the trade went against him.

As it turns out, Karim was not a very diligent trader and had not done his homework. The futures contract on JGBs is 10 million yen per contract. But Karim, without studying, thought that JGBs were denominated at 1 million yen per contract. Instead of trading $5 million position in JGBs, he found out later that he had put on a $50 million trade, ten times more than he had planned, consuming his entire account, and more, as collateral. The trade had immediately moved against him, delivering a steep loss from the get-go. As a result, at the end of the first day, Karim received a margin call. The brokerage called for him to immediately wire more money—over $1 million more—into the account. But Karim did not have it. The brokerage threatened to liquidate his position, which would have locked in his losses.

Karim frantically scrambled to add capital to his account so that he would not have to sell the position at a loss, which would have consumed all of his "hard-earned" money. But he did not have anymore. He called everyone he knew in order to borrow money to cover the margin call.

Over the next several business days, his short JGB position continued to deteriorate. Each uptick against him required more collateral. He was losing hundreds of thousands each day. Yet he had no remaining money of his own, so he had to call anyone and everyone he could to lend him the collateral to stay in the position until the unlikely day that it became profitable. Each friend who loaned him the collateral stood to lose all of their capital too as a result of helping him. It was a delicate walk. But Karim managed to get the capital he needed to keep from being liquidated in the hope that at some point the bonds would move back in his favor. Japan's markets do not open until the late evening Eastern Standard Time, so Karim was not sleeping a lot.

Luckily, four trading days later, a news event occurred that precipitated a significant drop in the price of JGBs. The price snapped back to the point that Karim not only recovered his losses but actually earned a profit. Profit, indeed. He pocketed $4 million. In a New York second,[1] Karim covered his short position in JGBs, suddenly four times richer than he was, if not twenty years older from the stress. I guess he showed *them*. Why be smart when you can be lucky?

There are three morals to this story. First, that someone has wealth does not necessarily mean that he also has intelligence. Second, never take risky positions that represent a superallocation of your portfolio. The third moral is know how to size your positions commensurate with your risk appetite (more on that below). Do not count on only one or only a few good ideas. Have many.

What about Karim? He went on to start his own fund and proceeded to lose the money of others by making similar mistakes due to lack of preparation and disproportionate position.

Know your securities thoroughly—no guessing.

So here are the rules. There are three basic ways to control the risk in your portfolio and to render the appropriate size per trade.

Equal Weight

Equal-weight portfolio construction is a perfectly valid risk-control tool, and it's simple. Divide the portfolio into

---

1. A New York second is the time between a traffic light turning green and getting beeped by the driver behind you. Years of personal research has shown it to be mere milliseconds.

equal dollar exposures for each target security, long and short. Rebalance your positions monthly or quarterly to maintain those exposures as intended. The rebalancing has the effect of taking gains out of your high winners and reinvesting in your laggards.

There is very good evidence of the value of putting equal weight to the positions in your portfolio. Determine in advance how many positions you would like to hold, say twenty; slice your available capital into twenty slots and allocate 1/20 of your dollars to each position. Rebalance as often as you prefer to keep each position in the portfolio of equal weight. I would do so monthly or quarterly. Don't be a snob; equal weight investing is very simple and effective. Moreover, you do not have to keep the number of positions constant. Change as often as you get good ideas and simply change the divisor.

The equal-weighted S&P 500 index (Rydex S&P Equal Weight; RSP) charted below, has looked pretty attractive compared to the capitalization-weighted S&P 500, which is the index that most people know. It is good evidence of the pragmatic efficacy of equal-weight investing. A capitalization-weighted portfolio is a methodology whereby the weight of capital allocated to any position is represented by the market cap of that security divided by the market cap of the entire portfolio. In spite of its simplicity, the equal-weight S&P 500 does quite well relative to the cap-weighted S&P 500. It often outperforms the cap-weighted S&P 500, which means that the equal weight also outperforms 85 percent of all long-only investment managers!

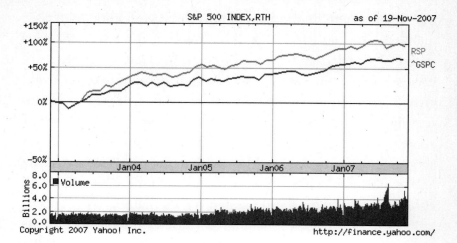

The obvious benefit of having an equal weight distribution is risk control. Sometimes, despite all of your research and rationale, some trades just don't work out. Equal weighting limits the size of your commitments to any one trade and will thereby limit the magnitude of a negative consequence from any one position. Of course, the upside may also be limited. In a portfolio of fifty positions, each position represents 2 percent of the portfolio on entering a trade. With only 2 percent of the portfolio allocated to any particular trade, even if the one position loses 100 percent (highly unlikely), the maximum influence on the total portfolio is only 2 percent. The upside is similarly limited, but having a collection of winners adds up.

Risk Baskets

Stepping up the sophistication just a notch, there is another way to organize your trades that gives some consideration to perceived risk. As before, pick the total positions into which you would invest your capital. In our examples, we have been using twenty stocks. Before you decide how much capital to place in any individual trade, organize all the potential trades into a list. Try to divide the list into three segments: high risk, medium risk, and low risk. The low-risk category will represent your tried-and-true, low-volatility trades that you are very sure will pay off. These are high-dividend stocks, solid growth companies, and solid macro trends. In the medium section, assign those positions that are lower in certainty but about which you have a strong feeling. The long-term slide in the value of the dollar could be such a trade; it is slow moving and long term but bound to reverse at any time. To the last and riskiest section, you should assign trades that are truly speculative, perhaps even event-related (based on announcements or earnings surprises), short term, or high risk. Assign weights to each group based on your own risk preferences—say, 50 percent, 40 percent, and 10 percent, respectively. Then equal weight the stocks within each group.

Long ago, in 1996, an investment club contacted me to give them some advice on how to get started. There were some members of the club who wanted to invest in the high-flying opportunities and were clashing hard against those who preferred to take a more conservative approach, emphasizing capital preservation. The rift was causing a problem with their portfolio inasmuch as decisions were not getting made, and the members were annoying one another. This was not a hedge fund by any means, but the mavericks of the bunch wanted to aggressively pursue hedge fund–like strategies.

I advised them to divide their capital into five categories, rated in terms of risk. My recollection is that, after some debate, their five categories turned out to be U.S. Large-Capitalization Stocks, Fixed Income (bonds), High-Yield Municipal, International Stocks, and Pure Speculation. I asked them to rebalance their allocations to each of these categories on a quarterly basis. In each category, they could purchase either mutual funds that represented the category or buy a group of individual securities that would align with each category.

This approach solved the problem of the members' disparate objectives. Each investor type was represented in at least one of the categories. The speculators had their own category to trade, pure speculation, as did the more conservative investors in the municipals and large-caps. I left the talk feeling a little guilty because I thought I had not provided anything sophisticated enough to have warranted their time. Years went by, and I forgot about them. Ten years later, I received a phone call, out of the blue. The president of the club called to thank me for the advice in retrospect. Like the Thermians in *Galaxy Quest*, they had followed my advice religiously and their portfolio blossomed as a balanced, risk-controlled vehicle for growth. They sidestepped all of the bubble madness in the early 2000s because they were hedged with fixed-income positions and not overexposed to any speculative bubbles. The speculative portion of their portfolio was restricted to 10 percent, so their risky exposures were relatively small—and profitable, as it were.

✓ Separating your target portfolio into risk categories is a strong, simple, and elegant way to control risk. The categories may change, but the structure is sound. In my own fund portfolio, an equity long/short strategy, options represent 10 to 20 percent of the total holdings, the riskiest component. The remaining 80 percent of the portfolio is allocated to stable, long-term, relative value, i.e., long/short equity hedges. If all the options expired worthless, i.e., expired unexecuted, I could lose as much as 10, 20 percent of the portfolio—good reason to keep that allocation small. But because the options book is well diversified, there are always some that are winning. And given the inherent leverage in options, one win often is all I need to enhance the profit on the entire book.

Risk Positioning

Stepping up one more rung, risk optimization is a sophisticated way to precisely target the risk limits of your trading strategy. The objective is to allocate your money based on the projected risk of each position, determined from historical performance measurement. You can look at each potential position's historic risk, as measured by the daily variability of the returns for each asset, and devise an allocation scheme, allocating more capital to less risky, stable assets and less capital to riskier assets. Instead of using your subjective assessment of risk, as we did with the risk baskets, you can use a specific, mathematical calculation. There is no guarantee that you will perform better than you would if you simply applied equal weight or risk baskets, but it does empower you with more insight regarding the expected risk/reward of your hedge portfolio.

The simplest way to manually "risk-size" a portfolio is to allocate capital in inverse proportion to the volatility of the security price. We measure volatility, or risk, by calculating the standard deviation of the security's historical returns. Standard deviation, in layman's terms, is the average change in the value of a security from one period to the next. The period can be a second, a minute, a day, or a month, and so on. The average change is measured both negatively and positively. If a stock had a value of $15 per share and its daily standard deviation was $12 per share, you might want to steer away because the magnitude of the volatility overshadows the price of the security.

If you have Microsoft Excel, you can use it to make the calculations. Excel has the basic functions to calculate standard deviation quite easily. If you don't have Excel, download StarOffice or open an account at docs.google.com to gain access to their online spreadsheet program. In order to calculate the daily standard deviation, you would array the daily return data series in the worksheet, and apply the standard deviation function. If you are not familiar with performing this calculation, it is worth taking the time to learn to do it.

Now that you have a measure of the periodic volatility for each target security, you can annualize it by multiplying by the square root of the number of your measurement periods that would occur in a year. If you reached the volatility calculation based on daily returns, you would multiply by the square root of 260, for the 260 trading days in a year. If your information was weekly, then you would multiply by the square root of 52, and so on.

, If the above makes sense to you, then great. If not, it may be easier for you to forget about the spreadsheet and instead look up the beta for each stock (www.finance.yahoo.com) and use the beta as the volatility datum. Beta is reported on finance.yahoo.com for every publicly traded stock.

If you measure risk by the first method, the spreadsheet method, calculate the reciprocal of the volatility for each position. If annual volatility (vol) = 20 percent, the reciprocal is 1 : 0.20 = 5.0. Calculate the reciprocal volatility number for each position to be optimized. In order to ascertain the optimal portfolio weight for any position, divide the security's reciprocal volatility number by the sum total of all the reciprocal volatilities, and that will represent the security's weight in the portfolio. For example, if the stock ABC has a volatility of 20 percent and the sum of all reciprocal volatilities in the portfolio is 100, then ABC's weight in the portfolio should be 5 : 100, or 5 percent.

If you are calculating risk based on beta, then divide each individual beta by the largest beta in the group. Again, calculate the reciprocals, and add all the adjusted reciprocal betas together. Then divide each security's individual revised beta by the sum total of all reciprocal beta's, and that will represent the security's weight in the portfolio. The one constraint is that the sum of all allocations should equal 100 percent.

Selling

Knowing when to sell is a most important discipline. It is one that few traders focus on. It's like learning to rollerblade. Everyone wants to learn how to go fast, but no one is interested in learning how to stop. Stopping is the most important skill of all. Similarly, most traders focus on finding the trade but are not nearly as diligent with respect to getting out.

Sometimes you hold a position because it has lost a lot of money but you still "like the company." The fair price of an asset could be significantly over or under the price at which it trades in the market. The fact that you like a company does not mean that its stock price is going to like you. Some of my very intelligent friends hold on to positions long after they have endured and sustained significant losses. "Well, it can't go anywhere but up from here," they reason. Even after they know that it is time to exit a dog of a position, they just don't want to give it up. Months later they are depressed because it has declined further or stagnated.

Occasionally, I do not drink my own Kool-Aid. Recently, I was faced with a sizable, more-than-anticipated return on a trade: It was up 100 percent plus. What next? In the fourth quarter of 2007, I was long a company called PetroChina (PTR) through American Depositary Receipts (ADRs). PTR raised US$8.94 billion from its initial public offering of A shares, making it China's largest domestic IPO to date. It had done well, so there were multiple reasons to keep the position. It yielded a dividend of 3 percent annually, which is a decent dividend yield, and it was well positioned versus the dollar, since its base currency was the yuan. In late 2007, oil was hitting nearly $100 a barrel, which was an historic high—further reasons for owning oil stocks. On the negative side, Warren Buffett was a huge investor in this company and had already sold all of his shares in October 2007 citing that it was overpriced. Contrarily, after his divestment, PTR stock advanced further upward.

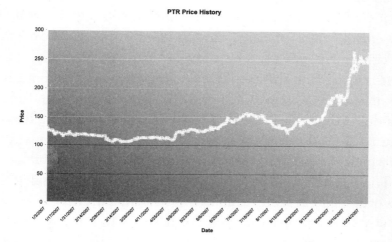

I invested in the position through the ADR at approximately $125 per share, and PTR promptly doubled in value in just a few months. The most recent months saw a particularly steep price increase because of the discovery of additional reserves and the company's raising of capital in the public equity markets for more exploration. "Should I keep it or sell it?" I wondered. My instincts said sell, but it was hard to carry through with it. "What if it doubles again?" I thought to myself. I got greedy.

Greed can obfuscate the path to good decisions. The responsibility for the control of (imprudent) greed falls on your shoulders. In hedge funds that job falls on the shoulders of the risk manager. The risk manager is the most vilified and sometimes the most hated representative in a hedge fund, from a trader's perspective. That is because the risk manager *must* reason and occasionally turn the lights out on a trade because of risk exposure.

As far as traders are concerned, the risk manager is not popular because he is usually the bearer of bad news. He does not give them enough time for their positions to become profitable. It is not uncommon to hear traders say, "Man, it was a great trade, but they cut me off before it could go to work. I was *only* down 30 percent. This place is terrible. How can you make money if you can't be allowed to lose occasionally?"

It is also often the case that traders are fired based on the risk manager's assessment. If you run your own hedge fund, you do not have the benefit of a risk manager breathing down your neck. You might, however, have a spouse who reins you in (which is a risk manager of a completely different sort).

There is no hard answer to the question of when to sell. On the other side of every transaction is someone who believes exactly the opposite that you do. If you sell, the guy on the other side of the trade is buying because he thinks that whatever it is you are selling is a good buy.

I should have sold out of the PTR position while the going was good. But it was going up and up, and I wanted to believe that it would do so forever. There were plenty of warning signs—not least of which was that Buffett had divested. Buffett divested because the IPO and future offerings would seriously dilute the investments of then-current shareholders—and *still* the stock went up. It was as if I had tetanus in my trigger finger—I couldn't click the mouse to sell it. There I was with all the other investors, all of us with the audacity of hope, thinking we could ride the price of the stock straight up into the stratosphere.

Wrong.

Any decision to transact a security—long or short—should have a price target. Once that target has been reached, unless there are compelling reasons to hold the stock, you should exit. Think to yourself, "If I were entering this trade today, would I still buy it." No? *Then get out!* Had I asked myself with PTR, "Gee, would I still buy it today? Would I invest new money in this position?" the answer would clearly have been no, and that should have been a sign to head quickly for the exit.

And I did. Sorta. Instead of selling the entire position, I sold two-thirds of my stock position at $262 per share. Then, rather than sell the rest of the position, I bought portfolio insurance by selling a call option against the entirety of the remaining position. The call option had a price of $29 per share. So in other words, I took in more than 10 percent of the remaining value of the position in a call premium. Selling a call option against a long equity position is called a covered call. Like a short, I took in $29 per share cash for selling the call option short, or 10 percent of the total position. Sweet! If the stock advanced further, it would have been called away from me at still a tidy profit. By taking in the premium, however, even if the position declined by as much as 10 percent, I still would have made a profitable trade: I would have taken in some cash, and would still own the stock, poised to enjoy the rest of the advance of PTR.

Great idea, but life is what happens when you've got other plans. The details of what happened in December 2008 went like this: As conditions would have it, the stock declined by more than 34 percent from a price of $262 to a price of $190, over the next few days. Given that I had taken in a premium of $29 per share, my loss on the remaining position was only 23 percent from the stock's high. It was still a very profitable trade over the holding period, but it was a precipitous loss from my decision point to keep it.

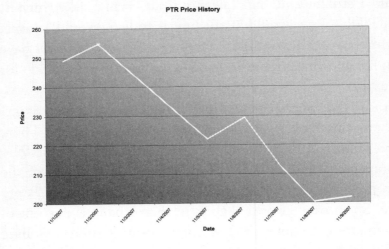

Once you have hit your performance targets and you've hit your happiness threshold return; sell.

Having said that, it is certainly okay to have long-term trades. In my portfolio, it is not uncommon for me to have a position for 100 to 150 trading days, which is more than half a year of trading days. If at any point during that term, however, if I can not justify entering the position that day at that day's price, then that position is a sell. Alternatively, I can always consider taking some of the profit off the table by selling off only a fraction of the position. The equal weight and risk baskets sizing disciplines would do that automatically, by the way.

One of the financial statistics I like to use to tell me when to enter or exit a stock is the PEG ratio. Peter Lynch popularized the PEG ratio years ago in the 1980s. "The P/E ratio of any company that's fairly priced will equal its growth rate." In other words, price divided by earnings equals growth.

The PEG ratio is just a number. That's all. There is no absolute value that makes it attractive or not. It is the relative value of the PEG ratio to that of other possible choices that is important, plus how it changes over time. If a company's stock has a PEG ratio that has been steadily declining, it's probably a sign that it's time to exit the position. If a company's PEG ratio is significantly lower than that of the overall market—say the S&P 500—and it has strong growth prospects, that may suggest an investment opportunity. Still, there are no absolutes here, some of it is art. Nevertheless, the PEG ratio is a very good guide.

The PEG ratio may be calculated by taking the stock's current price-to-earnings ratio and in turn dividing that by the growth expectations for the stock for the next twelve to sixty months. In principle, a PEG ratio with a value of 1 is a reasonable metric of the trade-off between the "cost" of a security (as expressed by the P/E ratio) and its growth prospects. Less than 1, and the company is attractive. More than 1, and the company could be overbought. Given the way valuations are today, you could wait months before you found a hedge opportunity beyond reproach if you used the absolute value of the PEG ratio as a guide. It is better to look at relative values. Perhaps two companies in the same sector with vastly different PEG ratios represent a great hedge. Buy the low PEG ratio and sell the high PEG ratio. I tend to look at a company's PEG relative to the S&P 500. If it is less than the S&P 500 in a sector I like, it is a buy. If it is more than the S&P 500, in a sector I hate, it is a short.

In summary, determine your exit targets *before* you get into a trade. Figure out how much of a trend you would like to capture based on your own assessments of macroeconomic changes. There are multiple ways to determine how much of your capital to risk in any one trade. We have investigated three of them. Variously, I use them all. Play around with your own mechanisms to match your risk tolerance.

CHAPTER 9

OVERVIEW OF HEDGE FUND STYLES

Devising your own hedge strategy is not going to be a cake-walk. There is a reason why great ability to trade sits in the hands of a relative few. Success *is* achievable, however, on a personal scale, given the free data resources available to you, your understanding of risk and how to reduce it, and your use of all available investment vehicles, particularly ETFs and specialist mutual funds, which significantly increases your ability to express your individual investment ideas.

As a first step, the homegrown hedge fund trader needs to identify his risk tolerance and return goals. Making money is everyone's objective, but it's helpful to know what you are willing to risk in order to achieve the profits you are seeking. Are you willing to lose all the money invested in your hedge strategy in order to yield great returns, or do you prefer a consistent, relatively low annual return with very little risk? Would you rather earn 12 percent annually with relative certainty or invest in a portfolio that has a 50 percent chance at a 40 percent return and a 50 percent chance at a –25 percent return? The second choice is more profitable over time, but the risk-adjusted returns and risk profiles are very different. Many investors would choose the first option because of its greater certainty of return.

The market scenario you choose speaks to your own risk preferences.

A safe way to toe the water is to allocate a relatively small portion of your investment funds to hedge trading. Start small and increase the allocations as your confidence grows and you will develop your own rhythm and style. Your account size is of less issue today. You can start by "hiring" your own traders by investing in ETFs. With the purchase of an ETF, these "personal traders" are on your payroll, working dutifully for you, expertly implementing your view of the markets. You can depend on their benchmark performance in your chosen concentration, whether that is U.S. growth companies or alternative clean-energy companies. They make sense for investing in themes and they are becoming increasingly popular even among hedge fund managers because they accomplish precisely what traders would do on their own: construct a basket of securities that would express their intended investment view.

Despite their reputation for being cowboys, most successful hedge fund managers—and even many of the unsuccessful ones—are quite rigorous and disciplined about minimizing risk in pursuit of their profit strategy. They make profits by mastering one strategy or style and executing it with precision, consistency, and skill. Their investors expect them to adhere to their avowed strategy. There are also hedge funds that are multimanager or multistrategy hedge funds, where the fund hires multiple in-house investment managers with a variety of styles. The result is a fund that in combination has a little exposure to a lot of different strategies. The diversification of alpha stabilizes the return of the fund because it always has exposure to a bull market, wherever it may exist. The well-known benefits of diversification similarly redound to the multimanager hedge fund.

The diversification inherent in multimanager funds makes them better arbiters of risk and reward. Compare the returns of a single-strategy independent hedge fund manager to those of a manager running the exact same strategy inside a multi-manager fund. The internal manager will generally have better performance. The reason is that the single-strategy external manager has a built-in fear factor. A bad quarter or bad month could disrupt the business model of a single-strategy hedge fund. Losses in the single-strategy fund could cause the external manager to face redemptions (from quick-trigger clients) and potentially delay the ability to raise additional capital for weeks or months. Potential investors will sit on the sidelines until a direction is clear.

The internal manager, on the other hand, is less concerned about the consequences of taking intelligent, defensible risks in his chosen strategy. His "bosses" and the risk manager understand risk thoroughly: they may even encourage the manager to take more risk if such additional risk complements the other strategies in the multimanager fund. A down month or two for a hedge strategy run inside a multihedge fund is less consequential because the multimanager fund does not depend upon one source of return. The manager can therefore take more intelligent risks and generate a better return profile. The single strategy manager is thus risk-averse compared to the internal manager.

Your hedge strategy should take the course of the multi-strategy fund. Diversify. Before you design your own strategy, it would be useful to decide where on the investment scale you would like to focus your efforts. Write it down: How much money? How much at risk? Which instruments? How often will you check your trades? Do you want the sexiness of running out of PTA meetings because you need to check your trades, or would you prefer to assess your strategy once a month?

Match up those preferences with the hedge fund styles defined below, and pick your disciplines. The hedge fund industry has established indices of performance for every style, so you can tell how you are doing in a particular strategy group relative to your peers, the professional managers (www. hedgeindex.com). These indices can help you decide the performance characteristics that are right for you.

Hedge Fund Styles

There are four major hedge funds styles: **Market Neutral, Long/Short Equity, Directional Trading**, and **Specialty Strategies**. The subspecialties of each major group further define the particulars of each style. These are the major styles and subspecialties, according to TASS Research:[1]

Market Neutral Group
Equity Market Neutral
Event-Driven
Market Neutral Arbitrage

Long/Short Equity Group
Aggressive Growth
Opportunistic
Short Selling
Value

Directional Trading Group
Futures
Macro
Market Timing

---

1. The categories are provided by TASS Research, including portions of the definitions.

Specialty Strategies Group
Emerging Markets
Income-
Multistrategy

Each of these strategies is a benchmark for your own trading. There is a good deal of overlap, and none of the rules for these groups is written in stone, but some styles will be better at meeting your objectives than others. "Better" can be described as the amount of return for the amount of risk, as commonly measured by the Sharpe Ratio. The Sharpe Ratio, or Sharpe, is a statistical measure of the quality of your return generation. Consistent, profitable strategies with little variability in profit/loss will generally have higher Sharpes. Highly variable strategies can also have high Sharpes, but their returns have to be very high to compensate for the higher risk. I favor the strategies with the highest Sharpe Ratios because you know that if all hell breaks loose, your account balance will remain relatively stable.

Below is the average monthly return performance since 2004 and the corresponding Sharpe Ratio for each of the four major hedge fund styles and their subgroups. A Sharpe Ratio greater than 1 means that for every unit of risk, you are adding at least the same amount of return over the risk-free rate. If the Sharpe Ratio of a strategy is less than 1, you are better off buying Treasury bills and taking a vacation than investing your money in those strategies. I do not intend to be obtuse except to suggest that the purpose of hedge trading is to maximize the Sharpe Ratio of your investing, which indicates that you are making good bets and taking intelligent risks.

Index / Substrategies	Average Monthly	Average Monthly Chg (+/-)	Sharpe
S&P 500	0.44%	2.36%	0.0
Market Neutral			
Convertible Arbitrage	0.36%	1.11%	**0.08**
Equity Market Neutral	0.66%	0.57%	**2.01**
Event Driven	0.96%	1.23%	**1.78**
Event Driven/Multistrategy	0.99%	1.52%	**1.50**
Risk Arbitrage	0.51%	0.91%	**0.65**
Distressed	0.96%	0.98%	**2.21**
Long/Short Equity			
Dedicated Short Bias	0.32%	3.86%	**-0.01**
Long/Short Equity	0.88%	1.83%	**1.04**
Specialty Strategies			
Emerging Markets	1.30%	2.21%	**1.52**
Fixed Income Arbitrage	0.40%	0.77%	**0.31**
Multistrategy	0.74%	1.12%	**1.27**
Directional Trading			
Global Macro	1.03%	1.16%	**2.10**
Managed Futures	0.53%	3.29%	**0.21**

Note that as a group, the market neutral strategies achieve the highest Sharpe Ratios on average. The market neutral strategies provide the most consistent and least variable returns month over month. Hedge strategies with low Sharpes have very devoted and very capable managers but, by construction and trading focus, are probably less hedged and experience greater variance in returns—you could be up one month and down as much the next. Managed futures, for example, an inherently directional, unhedged investment style, shows a Sharpe Ratio of only 0.21, suggesting that, on a stand-alone basis, there is little long-term value in investing in a managed futures program over simply buying Treasuries. You might be better off leaving your money in your savings account than allocating your capital to a stand-alone managed future strategy.

Similarly, not all of these strategies outperform the reward risk characteristics of the S&P 500 index. On a risk-adjusted basis, it could be a superior alternative to invest in a stock index mutual fund and just leave it alone. Go fishing. That does not mean that the S&P 500 will always outperform alternative strategies or vice versa. Over the last four years, the S&P 500 has had an average annual return of about 7 percent. You may find that investing in the stock market through a collection of equity mutual funds of various disciplines or even Treasuries is a better risk than some of the hedge alternatives. I just want to drive the point that the traditional strategies have value, too.

Below are brief descriptions of the hedge fund investment styles.

Market Neutral Group

The Market Neutral Group are a group of strategies that rely on relative-value hedges in the portfolio, being simultaneously long and short. Most of the examples in this book are market neutral hedges in which the portfolio is long one security and short another of like characteristics. These strategies are called market neutral because, as the name implies, the positions minimize the impact of broad market movements. The impact of the market's moves are hedged out by the portfolio being both long and short at the same time. These are the safest hedge strategies and tend to have the highest Sharpe

Ratios. The drawback is that it is a crowded discipline so relative-value spreads have been compressed. Simply put, it is more difficult to make the big returns. Market neutral managers have had to use other creative ways to earn the types of returns that hedge managers are famous for. These creative ways include using leverage and taking more risk exposure in the form of tilts long or short (partial hedges) or inherently riskier stocks.

Equity Market Neutral Strategies

This subspecialty of the Market Neutral Group is represented by many of the examples throughout this book. The strategy entails forming long and short positions that, when taken in aggregate, have no net exposure to the market. Managers invest equal dollar amounts in securities, both long and short, maintaining a portfolio with low net market exposure. The manager expects long positions to rise in value and short positions to decline, on a relative basis. The Deere/ConAgra hedge described in the last chapter is a typical example. When such a long/short hedge entails only two positions, it is called a pairs trade.

The selection of the long and short positions can vary based on multiple factors, including the company's fundamental value, its expected rate of growth, and the risk embedded in the security's price movement. Due to the portfolio's low net market exposure, performance is insulated from market volatility. If you select carefully, the direction of the market will not matter to your profit or loss. Expected returns are on the same scale as the expected average annual return of the stock market (9 to12 percent, unleveraged) but with only a fraction of the volatility.

Event-Driven Strategies

Technically, event-driven strategies are not market neutral at any one point in time. The manager will take a series of short-term, directional exposures based on news or other happenings with short-term effects on a stock. Maybe you have seen how a stock can trade off significantly when it misses an earnings expectation by one penny a share, or the Bear Stearns trade, where investors refused to believe that Bear would sell for $2 a share and pushed it up to $10. These are event-driven trades.

Typical "events" include earnings surprises, both good and bad: occasionally, stocks trade off significantly if a company announces great earnings, based on the "buy bad news, sell good news" adage a company may miss its profit targets. Precipitative events include announcements of spin-offs, mergers and acquisitions, bankruptcy reorganizations, recapitalizations, and share buybacks. Typical trades and instruments used may include long and short common and preferred stocks, debt securities, options, and credit default swaps.

Some traders program their trading engines to search online newsfeeds and automatically make trades based on information as soon as it is published. The intent is to "read" the news before anyone else does, then front-run the market's reaction. The trading engines do it faster than a human could.

Regardless, over time, in this kind of event-driven strategy, the manager aggregates a portfolio of positions based on specific situations evolving on a set of stocks. There is less specific attention given to balancing long and short positions. If the manager trades on both good and bad events, however, there will be market neutrality over time.

DISTRESSED SECURITIES

Distressed securities is a subset of the event-driven strategies. As in the broader Market Neutral Group, the manager takes long and short positions in stocks. The portfolio can often be concentrated. The manager buys companies that are on shaky financial footing, often by taking concentrated positions in stocks on which he can potentially exert influence. The manager may invest in either the debt or equity of companies in financial difficulty. Such companies are generally in bankruptcy reorganization or are emerging from bankruptcy, or appear likely to declare bankruptcy in the near future.

Under most circumstances, the manager is able to buy companies' securities at deeply discounted prices. If the company successfully returns to profitability, the company's stock price rises, providing a substantial profit to the manager. Recent large-scale examples of this strategy include the hedge fund Cerberus' acquisition of Chrysler or Ed Lampert's acquisition of Sears. Cerberus took over a majority interest in Chrysler Group $7.4 billion, from DaimlerChrysler, while Eddie Lampert risked $9 billion on the acquisition of Sears for $11.5 billion. But it is a tough business. Companies are distressed for a reason, which is why the risks are huge—but so are the profits when all works well. At this printing, the future of Chrysler is uncertain, as the company still teeters on the brink of bankruptcy, and Lampert has seen his Sears/Kmart merger lose 50 percent of its value from its high. The timetable to profitability on these trades is longer. The turnaround in a distressed company's fortunes can require an extended period of waiting time.

Merger Arbitrage

Merger arbitrage or risk arbitrage trades are driven by an impending merger or acquisition transaction. This strategy seeks to profit from companies undergoing acquisition as either targets or acquirers, or those preparing for a reorganization or spin-off.

Risk arbitrage opportunities are some of the most visible to the public. There is no real hidden opportunity, because the acquisition dynamics play out in full view of the public. The risk arbitrageur analyzes potential transactions based on his own number crunching and judgment. He will assess the price offer of the acquisition, as well as the probability of completion of the deal and the effectiveness of new management once the transaction is completed. On that basis, he will give the transaction a thumbs-up or thumbs-down.

If he believes in the transaction, he will purchase shares of the target company and generally hedge his position by taking a short position in the acquiring company. If he does not believe in the transaction, he will take the opposite positions or none at all.

The acquiring companies often pay large premiums for the target companies in order to stave off competitive bids and to ensure that the target company accepts their offer. Therein is the reason to purchase the shares of the acquiree—to capture the increase in share price from the current price to the published acquisition price. The shares of the acquiree will jump based on receiving such an offer. The acquiring company, on the other hand, assuming a successful consummation, will be saddled with significant debt. The acquirer is challenged with making the new, combined company work. The perceived difficulty in doing so is reflected in the short position on the acquirer.

In risk arbitrage, the trader is either bullish (long) on the deal (it will be successful) or bearish (short) on the deal (it will die). When Microsoft made a bid for Yahoo!, for example, for $33 per share, it was an offer at a significant premium to the trading price. Risk arbitrageurs immediately traded Yahoo!'s share price from $19 to $30 per share at the open of the next day. The trade up to $30 was not done stepwise: the stock gapped up in one jump, from $19 to $30. The risk arbitrageurs created a sort of auction at market open that was resolved by the market makers to a clearing price of $30 per share. In that trade, the only beneficiaries were those already holding the stock. But the fact that the risk arbitrageurs took the stock to only $30 and not $33 indicates that there remains some doubt as to whether the deal will complete. But the arbitrageurs are risking $30 to make $33, a 10 percent gain if the deal is consummated.

SPECIAL SITUATIONS

The special situations subspecialty is similar to the event-driven strategies except that the manager may use a wider range of instruments to take advantage of a perceived opportunity. Special situations is not well defined in the industry, but I think of it as event driven with multiple sources of profit, using such derivatives as credit default swaps or trading the balance sheet, which includes trading the debt and equity against each other in an event-driven play. For example, a great friend of mine was active in a company called Terryson.[2] When it went into bankruptcy, he bought both the equity and the debt at deep discounts. By owning both, he was able to get onto the reorganization committee and influence the best outcome for his investment. It worked. He's rich.

---

2. Not its actual name.

Other potential special situations include trading the effects of corporate restructurings (e.g., spin-offs, acquisitions), stock buybacks, bond upgrades, and earnings surprises.

Market Neutral Arbitrage

Market neutral arbitrage is the most quantitative strategy in the hedge fund industry. The Market Neutral Group is in search of mathematical patterns. The market neutral arbitrage manager may have no clue what his portfolio holds because positions are generally selected by automated processes facilitated by a computer. The turnover of positions—buying and selling—can be quite high, with some managers averaging as much as 100 percent a day.

The objective is to exploit inefficiencies in the market by constructing a hedged portfolio of long and short positions. The goal is similar to that of the market neutral fundamental hedge trader, except that the market neutral arbitrage trader uses primarily prices as his inputs—just pure quantitative analysis of prices movement and patterns.

The subcategories in this strategy include convertible arbitrage, capital structure arbitrage, and statistical arbitrage. Given the highly mathematical component of market neutral techniques, the barriers to entry have declined. Fundamental market neutral strategies have performed better in recent years than the pure quantitative models. In fast-changing times, the fixed computer models have proven more difficult to adjust than the human mind. The mathematics behind pure mathematical arbitrage is transferable and increasingly widely distributed. As a result, the margins—the profitability—for pure quant guys have suffered.

CONVERTIBLE ARBITRAGE

"Convert arb" is based on the same principles as the long/short hedge. In convert arb, the manager is long and short the same company at the same time in different financial instruments. The manager longs the convertible bond and shorts the company's underlying equity shares. The manager therefore buys one form of security he believes to be undervalued (usually the convertible bond) and sells short another security (usually the stock) of the same company. The hope is that the stock will advance sufficiently that the strike price of the convertible is triggered. It is a hedge in that the manager is long an equity-like instrument, the convertible bond, and short the equity.

The convertible bond is a bond with an embedded call option. The strike price for the convertible bond is the price at which it could be converted to a stock, or equity, position. When the convertible is issued, the price of the strike is already set in level and quantity, somewhat above the current trading price of the stock. If the stock never advances, the buyer still receives interest on the bond. If the stock price declines, the manager profits in two ways: interest on the bond and profit from the short stock position. If the market goes up substantially, the manager can exercise the call and convert the debt to equity profitably.

Convert arb is one of these strategies that experienced a dramatic deterioration in efficacy. The deterioration happened because hedge funds came to dominate the market (versus traditional investors), comprising virtually all the buyers and sellers for convertible debt securities. When a market is dominated by one type of buyer only, there is the strong possibility of a bubble, as they are passing the same securities back and forth to each other. As the amount of interested capital exceeded supply, investors paid higher premiums for the bonds, which led to drastically lower margins and high correlations.

FIXED INCOME ARBITRAGE

In this strategy, the manager takes long/short positions in fixed income securities and their derivatives in order to exploit interest rate–related opportunities. These fixed income securities are often backed by residential mortgages, and are known as mortgage-backed securities. The spreads can be profitable, but they tend to have a steplike payout. They are profitable until they aren't, and when they aren't, they can go the other way in a profound disastrous movement, especially the mortgage-backed securities.

The spread on fixed income is effectively shorting one fixed income instrument to buy the favorable interest rate of another. The market is not efficient, but it is intelligent. If there is an interest rate differential on fixed income, there is a reason for it—a gradient of perceived risk associated with the trade. In order to enhance profits, the hedge can consist of components of different credit quality. The carry trade can be extremely profitable as a cash cow until it isn't. Sell Treasuries and buy Brazil bonds—the interest rate differential can be very enticing; yet one great disturbance in the global fixed income markets can cause spreads to blow out and seriously hurt your pocketbook.

In the old days, the fixed income arbitrage strategy involved the differential pricing of, say, a ten-year bond and a thirty-year bond expiring in the future on the same date. Theoretically, given the then-current interest rate environment, the two bonds should trade at the same yield to maturity, assuming the credit quality is the same. Often they would not. The fixed income trader would arbitrage the difference. But as with many other quantitative strategies, this old-school type of arbitrage is not nearly as profitable as it once was. Technology made such mispricings easy to see and simpler to trade until the arbitrage no longer existed.

STATISTICAL ARBITRAGE

"Stat arb" is pure math and very few fundamentals. It is also inherently a very short-term trading horizon. Depending on the strategy, the hold time on a position may be as short as milliseconds. Access to data and the timeliness of the stat arb's response is critical. A trader sitting at the floor of the exchange receives data before the home trader sitting in the middle of Cleveland, even if the Clevelander has a real-time terminal like Reuters BridgeStation. The difference may only be a second, but in stat arb strategies, an extra second of market data may as well be an hour—it can make all the difference between a profit and loss. Stat arb strategies have evolved into being, in essence, as a result of electronic market making. If you have fatter pipes for market data, it is a significant advantage.

The proposition is this: Imagine two stocks in the same industry with similar characteristics and price performance, historically. If their stock prices get too far apart, the stat arbs will trade the difference to bring them back in line. It has less to do with fundamentals than it does calculating and trading the error between expected and observed stock movement. For example, consider a sector, say, Industrials. Historically, stock A and stock B tracked Industrials with near 100 percent correlation. When one goes up, they all go up, and when one goes down, they all go down. If, in the short-term, A, B, or the Industrial sector breaks out of the established pattern, the trader's computers will effect a trade to bring them back in line, knowing that they should have moved together. During a time period in which the Industrials sector and stock A move up 5 percent and stock B moves only 1 percent, the stat arb machine may effect a trade that shorts A and buys B with the expectation that at a minimum, B will show some upside performance and A may converge to B, based on historical performance.

Statistical arbitrage is inherently short term in nature, these opportunities are not visible to the naked eye and close sooner than a human could react manually. The turnover in the portfolio can approach 100 percent per day, so execution costs and clearing need to be pristine. It would be very difficult for the home-grown trader to execute this strategy profitably.

Long/Short Equity Group

Aggressive Growth

Long/Short Equity strategy is very accessible to the average investor. Long/short means that there is a hedge, but it is tilted to the long side or the short side, generally the former. The current excitement in the long/short equity space are the 130/30 strategies. 130/30 refers to being long 130 percent of your nominal investment and short 30 percent. The average investor can run a 130/30 portfolio in a typical brokerage account since it does not consume net leverage.

If a manager invests $10,000 in this type of strategy, he would buy $13,000 of stocks and short $3,000 of stocks. The net market exposure would still be $10,000, but the shorts provide some downside protection, while there is leverage (30 percent) applied to the longs. The 130 percent counts as leverage because you are buying $13,000 in securities while you have deposited only $10,000. The manager may consider a company's business fundamentals when investing and/or may invest in stocks on the basis of technical factors, such as stock price momentum.

The proposition is that the manager identifies companies that have great reason to grow in ensuing periods, balanced by strategic short positions. On the short side, the manager may choose stocks that are in out-of-favor sectors or that have fundamental statistics that do not warrant the current trade price.

Opportunistic

The Opportunistic strategy is an equity long/short strategy focused on short-term opportunities. Opportunistic trading strategies emphasize the purchase of undervalued securities or markets and the sale of overvalued securities or markets without the constraint of being fully hedged. This is another close cousin of the event-driven strategy, except that it can have significant directional tilts.

Short Selling

Dedicated short sellers maintain consistent net short exposure. Short sellers have nerves of steel. Honestly I do not know how they do it. The great majority of the time, they are losing money. For me, I have trouble swallowing my lunch if I am down even just one day, let alone every eight days out of ten.

To be a successful short seller, you must have fine-tuned forensic accounting talent. The dedicated short seller is, after all, betting against the opinion of the entire market. It takes great conviction and no fear; you will be losing money 80 percent of the time. Short sellers are the same guys who play "don't come" at the craps tables. It is a consistently, inherently negative approach. Dedicated short sellers find companies whose valuations they don't like, whose managements they don't like, whose business plans they don't like. They short as much of it as they can, and occasionally it becomes self-fulfilling. The statistics on finance.yahoo.com or shortsqueeze .com will tell you what percent of the company is short. When the market is sure that a company is a loser, the short rate can exceed 30 percent. But short sellers must be careful.

The short rates indicate how many days of average daily trade volume are necessary in order for the shorts to cover their positions. A short ratio greater than 5 may indicate a difficulty in exiting the trade profitably.

According to CSFB/Tremont, the monthly return of the Dedicated Short Bias Index was down 52 percent of the time from 2003 to 2007. Clearly, dedicated short selling has its challenges. A short can lose unlimited money (if the stock increases in value unabated), unlike buying a long position, where the loss is limited to 100 percent. If you short a stock at $1 and it goes to $5, then you've lost 500 percent of your money while the most a trader can profit on a short position, without leverage, is 100 percent. Moreover, shorts can be called in at any time, so you might have to close the position exactly when you would least want to. That is known as a short squeeze, evidenced by a spike in the stock price as short sellers desperately seek to cut their losses by buying the stock back. Short-selling managers typically target overvalued stocks, characterized by prices they believe are too high, given the fundamentals of the underlying companies. But the real sweet spot is companies whose accounting is furtive, hiding potentially damaging information about their financial health.

Directional Trading Group

Futures

Futures traders employ a broad group of strategies. The investment objectives are very diverse. Typically a futures trading strategy exhibits a high degree of directional bets with respect to countries (equities), sovereign debt, currencies, and commodities—not with individual companies. From a global macro perspective, the futures trader will make tactical allocations to high-level global, or macro themes. If a country's GNP is expected to grow, the trader will buy futures represented by the *entire* stock market, not just one security. If there is a spread in growth expected in, say, Europe versus the United States, the trader will buy the *entire* European stock market and sell futures for the entire U.S. market (S&P 500 futures)—the equivalent of being short the market. Or, for example, the manager may hold long positions in the U.S. dollar and Japanese equity indices while shorting the euro and U.S. Treasury bills.

Futures traders coined the phrase "The trend is your friend." Their opportunities come from slow-moving global macroeconomic trends and tend to be longer term in duration. The negative side of trading trends is the crowd mentality. A trend trade is like a New York cocktail party. People may show up throughout the night, some early and some fashionably late, and all have a great time and get drunk on the punch. But when the lights go out and the party is over, everyone hits the exit at the same time. The line at the coat check can be long and raucous. And you might not get your coat back. That's why Directional Trading Groups have such low Sharpe Ratios.

As a result of trading popular trends, futures trading has rarely yielded a Sharpe Ratio in excess of the S&P 500. In our table at the beginning of the chapter, you'll see the Sharpe Ratio of futures trading is a paltry 0.21, the lowest of any of the hedge strategies. The S&P 500 has a Sharpe of 0.0 for the same period, and a higher return to boot! It is hard to make a case for employing a pure futures strategy. Futures strategies provide their best value as a component of a diversified hedge fund. Futures trading has a relatively low correlation to many other hedge fund strategies, so it can add value to the overall portfolio containing several hedge fund styles. Even a strategy with a zero return can improve the reward/risk characteristics of your overall portfolio if the strategy is uncorrelated.

The Futures category would generally include global macro,

in which the manager constructs his portfolio based on a top-down view of global economic trends, considering factors such as interest rates, economic policies, inflation, etc. Rather than considering how individual corporate securities may fare, the manager seeks to profit from changes in the value of entire asset classes.

Specialty Strategies Group

Emerging Markets

Globalization has generally benefited the emerging markets as developed nations continue to pour money and investments into developing nations. China and India have represented an especially great trend. The emerging-markets trader invests in securities issued by businesses in and/or the governments of developing countries, loosely determined by per capita GNP. Emerging market examples include Brazil, China, India, and Russia. The manager may invest in any asset class (equities, bonds, currencies) and may construct his portfolio on any basis (value, growth, arbitrage). An individual investor, can get great access to the emerging markets through the ETFs.

As would be expected, the emerging markets can be volatile and require particular care. Risk in these markets is more than just the variability of day-to-day returns. Other significant forms of risk include liquidity, political risk, currency risk, etc. Hugo Chávez says something crazy, and the consequences can reverberate through all of the Latin American emerging markets. Recently he amassed troops on the border of Chile and then just as abruptly pulled them away. I can assure you that the sales of Tums to emerging-markets traders were at an all-time high. These markets can have you elated on the way up, but they are hypersensitive to news. Those great profits can melt away in a heartbeat.

It is a misnomer to call the emerging-markets style a hedge strategy. It can be difficult but not impossible to short in the emerging markets. There are usually not enough buyers to "lend" individual stocks to in order to make a short sale and therefore create the classic hedges we have discussed. Given the high correlation between the developed and emerging markets, the hedge trader in the emerging markets can use ETFs of the developed markets as a hedge, such as the SPDR S&P 500 (SPY) and the iShares FTSE 100 (ISF:LN) ETFs. Since the risks vary between these markets, you might not use a fully dollar-neutral hedge. If you beta-weight the hedges, they would likely be greater in dollar volume than the emerging markets. For example, if you are long 100 in, say, Venezuela, you can short 120 in SPY.

Multistrategy

The multistrategy approach is the real answer to constructing a viable long-term hedge strategy. Multistrategy funds tend to be the most consistent because not only do they have exposure to multiple investment styles, they also can change the weighting of any individual strategy according to that which performs. It is not realistic for the average investor to run independent hedge books in each of the hedge fund styles and to risk-weight them according to current outlook. But it is possible to express multiple hedge views in your portfolio that capture a range of opportunities in the hedge universe. A word of advice: research[3] demonstrates that the difference between the top-performing multistrategy funds and the lowest-performing multistrategy funds is directly proportional to their exposure to the Market Neutral Group. Those with higher exposure do well; those with lower exposures have

---

3. Andrew Weisman, Merrill Lynch Hedge Fund Development Group.

greater volatility and smaller returns. That confirms the numbers in our Sharpe table.

What Does It All Mean?

Though this overview of styles may not have been the most exciting, you are now in a position to take the torch and do your own research to determine the strategy or strategies best suited to your own style and objectives. Generally, managers adhere pretty closely to these styles because they align with the strengths of the manager. The first strategies I developed were based in statistical arbitrage because I was impressed by the rigor and approachability of structured mathematical strategies. It fit my personality. I could program, and the strategy had a return profile that I thought, in 1999, would be a strong value proposition for potential customers. (I was wrong. What investors really wanted was Internet stocks.).

After all is said and done, do what plays to your strengths, and most important, use the strategy that makes investing fun. Man does not live by bread alone; he's gotta have some "moosarella" too.

CHAPTER 10

TALES FROM THE CRYPT

From the outside, the hedge fund industry must seem like a strange playground. Aside from the vast sums of money that hedge fund mavericks and masters manage, there is the way they attain their vast wealth that is so intriguing. And the successful ones are very wealthy. We live in an era when the news media reports on a newly minted billionaire, and it elicits an apathetic shrug: "He's not *that* rich." Being a billionaire doesn't carry the "wow" factor it once did.

A friend of a friend, a lawyer, was an early employee of Google. She retained 1 percent of Google for her service to the company. When the company went public, she became an instant billionaire. Today she is worth more than $3 billion, just because she did her job. It was an amazing windfall. There are a lot of lawyers who work a lot harder. Still, she deserved it because she was there from the start. I believe that. To put it into perspective, though, the CEO of the hedge fund I once traded for, a well-regarded trader, earns close to $1 billion **per year**, conservatively.[1] That is a lot of cake.

---

1. No names. It is better to sail stealthily under the radar.

Billion Is the New Million

I am hardly an insider. The fortunes of my fund, a long/ short equity fund, has hovered in the lower end of the industry assets, with peak assets of about $200 million. In relation to the rest of the industry, this makes me a pauper. I cannot really be considered a "player" at that size. I am the Brad Gilbert of hedge funds. I have mostly been an independent manager, but I have also had extended professional assignments inside other hedge funds, some of them quite large and "best of breed."

During my most recent experience in a large hedge fund, one of the things I noticed first was the lack of activity on the trading floor. It was one of the largest hedge funds in the world. The offices were spacious and comfortable and really *really* quiet. It was nothing like the trading floor caricatures you see in the movies. You could almost hear a pin drop on the trading floor. One reason is that there were a lot of empty seats. At any moment, twenty-four hours a day, the firm was actively throwing $40 to $80 billion (including leverage) around the markets globally, but you would hardly know it. The business has changed rapidly, facilitated by technology advances in telecom, data streams, and automation for high-velocity trade execution.

Technology not only made it unnecessary to talk to each other, it also made it unnecessary to even show up. Everyone silently used Instant Messenger to make trades. Further, why sit in an office chair where the air-conditioning is too cold or uncomfortable when one could be sunning on the beaches of Bridgehampton or Miami, checking the market and making trades from specially fitted BlackBerries?

There is a pecking order amongst hedge managers that derives directly from the maxim "Size matters." I got my first lesson in the pecking order in a humble epiphany that "Gee,

I wish I were bigger." One day I needed the help of one of the IT guys who was working at the trading station of one of the senior traders. I was also a senior trader, but I learned that there is senior and there is SENIOR. The other senior trader was not more experienced or more capable than I was (I say this with all modesty), but he was running a *lot* more money than I was, about $3 billion.

Bored of standing, I sat down at the senior trader's workstation. Innocently, I looked over at his day's profit and loss statement (p&l).[2] I admit I was curious because I had, in fact, done well that day, and I wanted to see how I stacked up. My book[3] was up around about 30 basis points, or 0.30 percent for the day, which is not bad for a day's work. I made $300,000 for the firm. Yea! In fact, I was proud of it—that was a pretty good day in the stat arb world. The senior trader was running a different strategy, a long-biased portfolio (mostly long positions, some short). I glanced sidelong at the performance stats on his flat screen. I nearly cursed out loud; he was up more than I was, about 80 basis points.

What astonished me next was not the magnitude of his earnings in percentage terms but in absolute dollar terms both for himself and for the firm. He had made $24,000,000 for the firm that day, a slow day, a summer Friday. Jeez! But even more striking was his personal take of the profits. Right on the screen he tabulated (as he apparently did each day) his personal take in the profits. On this slow summer day his earnings were $4,800,000. For *just one* day! And for performing only 80 basis points! Imagine being in a job where the daily variation in your *personal* account is $5 million. If he

---

2. Profit and loss statements show the excess of all gains (realized and unrealized), income, dividends, and interest income attributable to the trader's account over all expenses and losses (realized and unrealized).
3. Trading account.

made just 10 percent for the firm by the end of the year, his bonus would be $60 million . . . *every year.* And he was just one of many traders at the firm. That is why everybody wants to be in the hedge fund industry.

To make matters worse, the senior trader was a really nice guy. You would never have known that this was the scale of his daily remunerations. Sometimes he probably *lost* $5 million personally, but I doubt the daily variation had a serious impact on his lunch money. He was one of the most humble, patient, nicest guys around. Yet after that day, for some reason, I did not like him very much anymore.

Starting a Fund

Naturally, you might be curious about what it takes to start a fund. Starting up a hedge fund is very challenging. You are either starving or you are rich. It is pretty binary.

I once co-managed a hedge fund with a man named Joseph. He was a real nasty fellow. Really nasty. I never really "got" most of the programming on Lifetime Television until this partnership. I experienced firsthand what it was like to be in an emotionally abusive relationship. We had decided to start this enterprise together, so I was dependent on him and he on me. When you learn that someone is a monster, you have two choices: kill him (which is illegal) or leave him, which is tough if you are financially interdependent. Quietly, I planned my exit—but not until we raised some money.

Getting the first $50 million in a hedge fund as an unknown (as we were at the time) is very tough. You have to turn every stone and take capital wherever it is available. We raised money from an odd lot of peculiar, fast-trigger early investors. One such investor was an entrepreneur who had recently sold his company for $80 million. He was now rich after years of struggle, and he was eager to get richer. For him, a hedge fund was some kind of black box that you plugged into a wall, and money spit out the other side. We did not want to burst his bubble and were eager to be his black box. He was deep into pursuing the privileges of his newfound wealth.

When the investor came to New York, he suggested we meet on his turf. He invited my partner to meet him in his hotel room. Joseph and I prepared assiduously for the presentation, expecting to be grilled on matters of high finance. When Joseph arrived, however, he was stunned at the scene in the "presentation" room.

"It was one of the weirdest meetings I have ever presented at," he told me afterwards. "The whole time I was pitching the fund, he had three girls in the room—one was straddling him, grinding his torso; one was sitting on his face; and the other in the corner pleasuring herself, all on the payroll."

The investor was in a good mood though. He wrote us a check for $8 million.

One of our other early investors was an Asian billionaire. We found him as a result of a tip from one of my friends at the investment banks. This particular investor was savvy and understood hedge funds very well, as well as the business of intelligent risk taking. He was not fearful of young funds and even favored investing in young, promising hedge managers. I set up a meeting.

I had recently read an article about Carlos Slim, the richest man in the world—worth $59 billion (more than Bill Gates and Warren Buffett). Slim was famous for his thriftiness, showing up at business meetings in modest clothing, and wearing a cheap calculator watch.[4] This Asian investor, who was from old-money money, had a similar appearance. We did not know that in advance.

---

4. *Forbes*, August 6, 2007, "Carlos Slim, the Richest Man in the World."

We were very excited about the meeting and spent days readying our offices on Park Avenue. We bought tony tea sets and plates and cutlery and flowers. We polished our shoes and manicured our hands (and feet).

On the day the investor came to visit, he threw us a curveball and showed up early. Our receptionist was out on an errand, so he simply walked into the office unimpeded and ungreeted. This was, without a doubt, an instrument of his due diligence, to see what we were like when we weren't expecting anyone.

The investor looked disheveled, and Joseph, being a hothead, chided him and shooed him back into the hallway. "We didn't order anything," Joseph snapped. Just before the door closed in his face, the investor asked for us by name, and it became clear, embarrassingly, that this man who Joseph had assumed was a delivery boy was actually the investor for whom we had hoped to appear genteel.

Mr. Asia had on a disarming disguise. He was a thin, diminutive man. He wore pants that were visibly worn in the seat and knees and were several sizes too big. He cinched his belt supertight. His shoes were well traveled, and he was balding, with a wisp of hair that stood straight up, begging for a comb. He was also very intelligent, genial, polite, and circumspect. We were nonplussed, to say the least, but managed to present to him informally in an extended four-hour conversation regarding our view of the global markets. He nodded and stayed mostly silent. By the end of the meeting, we had earned his investment and his respect. And so it was. We were in business.

Your Broker Is Not Your Friend

Brokers are very important. Your broker is your hired professional servant, your window to timely and privileged market information. He is highly paid;[5] feel free to use your broker for information. He owes it to you. Call him often. Ask to speak to the company's analysts. Tell him to get you information. It is his job to make sure you have everything you need in terms of data, strategy, information, and help with execution. He is a valued and necessary asset—but he is not your friend, because his earnings are a function of a zero-sum proposition: I win; you lose.

In the early days, I was an adviser to hedge funds, subcontracting statistical arbitrage techniques to any fund that wanted to deploy it. One of those clients was a trader, Fernando, who learned the guile of brokers to his own ruin.

Fernando was new to the industry and confident, but he was a very poor trader. He quickly learned that hedging is the hardest part of a hedge strategy. Successful trading is not as easy and glamorous as it looks; like most successes, it takes hard work.

Fernando placed mostly directional bets, so his trading results were volatile. Luckily for me, there were a lot of macro traders who had high-volatility profiles (a euphemism for "loses money a lot") and sought the stability of low-volatility strategies as a complement. Fernando engaged me to subadvise portions of his young fund because he was interested in reducing the p&l swings from his own undisciplined investment strategies. The thought was that as long as he had one of these "low-volume" engines running in the background, it would create some stability in his portfolio.

I was running a statistical arbitrage that was profitable, but given that it was a black box, it was difficult to earn trust despite my stat arb's demonstrated performance. So I only man-

---

5. I am amazed at how the investment banks "fee" your account. In my own "high net worth" account at one of the banks, the sheer creativity and stealth of the fees was impressive.

aged a minority of the fund. Fernando lost money and earned money, with great swings in p&l. It was a sufficiently wild ride that he could scarcely keep an execution trader at his firm. The execution trader is the person who actually executes and administers the trades made by the portfolio manager or senior trader. The execution trader is the one who actually talks to the broker(s) at the exchanges. Because he was often shorthanded, I would sometimes help Fernando because he was not always able to work the brokers himself. (That should have been a glaring warning sign. What capable trader does not have a razor-sharp understanding of his net positions?)

Fernando would trade *everything*—futures on currencies, sovereign debt, and equity markets, in just about any country that had a futures market. Futures offered a lot of leverage, so the daily p&l had a *lot* of lumps in it. The path of Fernando's profit and loss throughout just one day was an internecine drama of twists and turns that would make your head spin. He seemed to have an appetite for destruction, and it would put my stomach in knots to see the swings. My own stat arb strategy was boring but chugged along profitably and managed to provide some of the yin he was looking for, relative to his yang.

When no one else was there (or refused to administer to Fernando), I interacted with the brokers. It was kind of a new experience actually talking, since stat arb required no human interaction whatsoever. But it was fun, speaking. I highly recommend it. Sometimes, the broker would stop by the office to take Fernando out to dinner or lavish him with tickets to sporting events and music concerts. I initially thought it strange that a broker would give him such attention, but I soon realized that the frenetic volume of Fernando's trading alone generated $200,000 annually for the broker in *net* commissions. Fernando was a broker's friend indeed. Whether you liked Fernando or not, he was a guy you wanted as a customer, even though he had a hair-trigger temper and frequently flew into rages.

One broker explained it to me this way. "He can yell all he wants. I can take it. He can call me names. He can curse my mother. Just as long as he pays me." Of this particular broker, I will say that I had never seen anyone willingly take so much verbal abuse. I empathized. Fernando called it "conditioning the broker" because without the abuse, he determined in his own inimitable way, the brokers would feel comfortable "cheating" him. He knew that being cheated was ostensibly unavoidable, but he felt it was essential to keep his brokers scared to keep it to a minimum.

I once found myself on the phone with one of Fernando's primary broker/traders after Fernando had given him a severe tongue-lashing. I had called him to see what was up and to make sure he understood this was just the way Fernando did business. Surprisingly, the broker was unperturbed. I knew he had thick skin, but this was disproportionate even for him.

"Wayne, let me tell you something," he said. "I have been on the floor of the exchange for a long time. Customers come and customers go. After a while, you begin to get a nose for who will make money and who will lose money. And you can tell right from the jump.

"Most global macro traders lose money," he continued. "Some take longer than others, but eventually they lose enough to force them out of business. It could take two weeks, two months, or two years. But I can identify them a mile away. A loser is obvious from the start."

"I hear you," I retorted. "But Fernando is really good. He really knows his stuff."

"Wayne, Fernando is one of the guys who loses money. He trades thousands of contracts a day, in and out. When he calls me to make a trade, I give him whatever execution price he asks for, even if it doesn't print. If the bid/ask is trading at 1.25/9, I buy it for him at 1.25. The irony is that it earns me chits with him because he thinks I am doing him a favor. The truth is that when I hang up the phone, I don't even place the order. I just say, 'Yep.' Instead of making the trade, I just journal the trade manually into his account, cuz I know he is going to lose money. Later, when he trades out of the position, I manually enter a closing journal entry and take the losses from his account and place them as profits in my own trading account."

I was aghast. We were, after all, on a recorded line. I hung up. For months I had tried to figure out why he was always so calm under the pressure of being Fernando's trade partner. Now I knew. Fernando's trading style and resultant losses were his gain, on *top* of the commissions. What a ruse.

You and the broker play a zero-sum game. He is your professional asset and not your friend.

The broker? His firm? Down in flames. But not before Fernando.

You Are a Paparazzo

No matter how big your own fund gets or even if you are managing money for an investment club or other source of capital, keep in mind that the capital markets are vast. The total worldwide equity market is around $50 trillion. That's a lot of money. Understand that whatever brilliant strategy you have conjured, it has been thought of before, is actively expressed in the market, and is probably better implemented somewhere else.

If you do start to get it right with your trades, please do not suffer delusions of your own genius. Do not let your guard down and start to take more risks simply because historically you have had successes. The markets do not know you and, like a rabid pet, will turn around to bite you at any moment.

The only players who can truly influence the market are trading in volumes of cash that are incomprehensible to the average person. Every value you are finding is profitable because it was found by a lot more capital than yours.

Therefore, you are riding in the wagon of the big boys. Know that it could turn on a dime. For example, Apple and a few other tech stocks were responsible for 70 percent of the NASDAQ rebound in 2007. That was a great trade, particularly if you "discovered" it as a result of your market savvy. But by the end of January 2008, they had traded off 50 percent. Do you believe that there was any fundamental difference in the companies and their prospects between December and January? Of course not. It was the intelligent capital reallocating and trading out for the next bang. There is nothing you can do about it except ride the wave while it crests and try not to ride so long that you wipe out.

Trading is a Thrasymachean universe, so people are going to make money any way they can. One of two things will happen. Either they will get regulated out of their game, or eventually others will catch on until there are scant profit margins to be had. This is why people trade on inside information or try to scam mutual funds (mutual fund timing[6]). The struggle and competition to get a leg up is fierce.

During the tech days, there were funds set up simply to churn trades—literally buying a security and simultaneously selling it. The cost of doing the trade would be the bid/ask spread and the cost of commissions, which was exactly the point. These special-purpose hedge funds were specifically

---

6. A illegal practice whereby traders attempt to gain short-term profits through illicitly buying and selling mutual funds at yesterday's price.

set up to make specious round-trip trades to earn trade volume with the investment banks. The objective was to execute enough volume to be rewarded with hot IPO allocations. The investment banks would allocate IPOs to their best (i.e., highest volume) customers, and these special trading vehicles were a way to ensure that the fund would always get a fresh stream of IPOs it could later flip at substantially higher prices to the unsuspecting John Q. Public. Greed and creativity are chummy bedfellows, and creativity does not always fall on the side of ethical behavior or the side of the smaller investor.

I knew a trader who influenced the market with volatility at the close in order to steal (burgle is probably a better word, as his activities were stealthy and clever) a profit—repeatedly, often, and in size. He made so much money at it, in fact, that the NYSE became aware of the practice and changed the rules for "market on close."

The trader, let's call him Adam, would buy call options into the close in size, buy the same securities in the cash market, then exercise the options for cash profit. He would effect an end-of-day arbitrage that would net him huge profits, and you, the small investor, would get hosed because you couldn't even see such maneuvers.

Let me explain in a little more detail. Briefly, if the options were within a few days of expiration, there was very little premium left. He would buy $100 million or more in the S&P 100 Index (OEX) calendar call spread, buying the call option near expiration and selling short the far call. Since a trade on the OEX Index is considered a cash settlement, he would spend $25 million or so buying individual stocks of the OEX into the close. He would be willing to "spend" the $25 million in order to trick the market into thinking there was high demand in the market, all the while increasing the value of the call options.

The futures market would essentially be settled so there would be little reaction. Once the index had moved sufficiently, he would exercise the index futures calls, taking in a very handsome profit just by creating a little volatility at the end of the day. The small trader, you, wouldn't even notice that Thomas just vigged $50 million in profits from you in the market's closing seconds. The only thing you would have noticed was a late surge in the market that benefited your long portfolio. And you would have thought, "Wow, I made a good call today."

⟩ My point is that professionals are squeezing everything they can out of the market *all the time*. Every normal idea has been had, so they are doing things that are invisible to you but that have an impact on your money. Be aware that every great idea you have is just a ripple in a much larger wave. Do not be deluded by the magnitude of your own success. Hubris is a real affliction. Be diligent. Be prudent. Be nimble.

"Turn the Machines Back On!"

I have witnessed some nasty meltdowns firsthand. They are fascinating things to watch. Meltdowns result from a paradoxical commitment to a trade or idea beyond personal solvency. It is holding on to hopeless positions or methods.

In his book *No Bull*, Michael Steinhardt relates how he would occasionally wake up in the morning and just hate every position he was in. He would go to the office and sell everything for cash. Then he would inform his analysts of his decision (which I am certain made them very unhappy) and challenge them to come up with new ideas. Sometimes hitting the "refresh" or "do-over" button is essential for generating profitable fresh ideas. Do not become committed to anything other than your own capital preservation and growth.

When I was ten, I remember having saved $50 for the first

time. Flush with cash, I went to the local fair mostly to walk around, inebriated with the power of discretionary dollars in my pocket. I had no intention of spending anything. It just felt good that I could if I wanted to. One of the vendors hissed a professional "Pssssst" in my direction to invite me to play the game he was working. I was hesitant, but he offered to start me off with a substantial discount to the regular price. It was a pin and ball game where the player would push a wooden ball on a string past a bowling pin in such a way that upon its return, it would knock the pin over.

The first three tries were a dollar, and then the price went up incrementally with each successive round. Despite what I believed was great hand-eye coordination, I simply couldn't get it. I nervously lost nearly half of my money and became resigned and tried to quit. But the vendor goaded me on, telling me how simple the game was and assuring me of the likelihood of reclaiming all my losses. He even turned the bowling pin upside down, feeling sorry for me, so that the wide end was at the top to make it easy. I still could not do it. Like the hamster hitting the lever to deliver drugs to his brain, I kept trying the same trick, over and over again, with the same losing result until all my money was gone. I was crestfallen, but it was an early lesson. The vendor felt sorry for me, but he still took my money. Take your losses early and move on.

One of the first times I saw a fund wipe out was when I was working in a hedge fund hotel. Hedge fund hotels are offices set up by the brokerage firms so that young funds can get up and running immediately, without having to worry about setting up the Internet, phones, support personnel, trade execution, etc. I was sitting next to a global macro trader, Stephen, who idolized the hedge fund Market Wizards. He had many stories about his brushes with George Soros, Stanley Druckenmiller, Louis Moore Bacon, Julian Robertson, and the like. He read every book he could on hedge fund traders and their methods. He was obsessed.

Stephen appeared to know his craft. He traded futures and specialized in "punching his profits through" by picking off market buyers and sellers in futures, trading one off the other. These were darting, high-turnover trades executed with two phones at his ear. He would, for example, trade a security in one ear and work the countertrade in the other ear. He would hold the brokers on the line while they gave a continuous stream of market quotes until one of the brokers misquoted a price. "DONE!" he would say and subsequently off-load the same future to the broker/trader in the other ear, making a riskless profit. That's how he built house money for the month. It was pedestrian, but he was a market-maker of sorts. He would commence each month with these kinds of trades to cover the rent. Once covered, he could focus on other market opportunities.

Bored with the nickel-and-dime game, he was convinced one summer that the market was going to go up strongly, based upon research he had read. He decided that he was going to bet heavily. "It just seems ripe," he told me.

Stephen made huge long bets on S&P 500 futures. Inherent in futures is 20 to 1 leverage. If, for example, you have $10 million you can make $200 million in bets without further collateral. He had "big bank" at risk.

Well, the very next day, the market tanked. It tanked and it tanked huge. In the first wave, the market was off as much as 5 percent by midday, wiping out most of his account and his wealth. Knowing the impact it had had on his p&l, you would have expected him to sulk or be dejected. In a perverse display of the Stockholm syndrome he was, instead, euphoric. Each tick down cost him millions, yet he expressed with glee that the "big boys," the Market Wizards whom he idolized, were taking this market down "like a Jersey girl."

"Go boys, go!" he screamed at his monitor as if he were at the racetrack. He cried and laughed simultaneously with happy adulation that his "mentors" were showing their market might while his life savings and the substantial investments of his clients were evaporating.

Mercifully, in the late afternoon, the market took a breather from its cruel and merciless decline. I expected him to take this chance to exit the market so he would have some pennies to bet more wisely on another day. He picked up the phone. I thought for sure that he was calling the broker to tell him to sell his positions, based on the temporary bounce. He did just the opposite. Instead, he took whatever buying power was left in his account and doubled down, secure in his conviction that this was an even *better* opportunity to make the trade work.

Not more than a few seconds passed before the market started again on its wild ride, this time in the right direction. The market had a dead-cat bounce and was beginning to show some momentum to the upside. He was visibly vindicated. He waited anxiously for further market advances as he cheered on his trade. He was convinced the Masters had taken the market lower so that they could reenter at a lower price. This was his chance to ride in their wagon and drink their Kool-Aid.

The positive reversal did not last for long, however. Like a lightning bolt, the market began to crater even more aggressively. It was as if there was not a single person in the universe who wanted to buy a share. The market was dropping like a ton of bricks, Stephen's fortune and his investors' fortunes with it. Red and more red filled the screens, the numbers dancing wildly with a surge of intensity from each downward plunge.

"The boys! My boys!!" he shouted with an eerie combination of delight and fright.

And so the bloodbath continued until the closing bell rang on the futures market at 4:15 p.m.

The exhaustion and sadness afterwards reminded me of the Duke brothers in *Trading Places*, Randolph and Mortimer, begging for the Exchange to turn the machines back on. Stephen was wiped out. On cue, his fiancée (blond, beautiful, skinny and, as usual, with several shopping bags in her hands) made an unannounced visit to the trading floor (she knew never to come before 4 p.m.) to show off her "finds," the lavish purchases she had made that day. Stephen struggled to project a lightness of being. I was impressed with the happy timbre of his voice, knowing, as I did, what just happened.

"Hi, honey! How are youuuuuu?" he chimed. It was a stunning display of emotional hegemony. Stephen feigned confidence as if nothing had happened. But from that night on, he was broke.

Take your losses early. Regroup. Move on.

The Folly of Seeking "A" but Rewarding "B"

One of my trader colleagues, Barry, used to run the proprietary trading desk at one of the major investment banks. He proposes that risky behavior among traders is inevitable, particularly at the investment houses, not the hedge funds.

"Wayne, you are running a hedge fund business, and you can ill afford any impropriety or style drift in the way you run money. It would put your whole business at risk. Not so at the investment banks."

Barry claims that risk-seeking behavior is not impelled by hedge funds' compensation structure. To the contrary, it is the investment houses that incite risk-seeking behavior, precisely because such economic incentives do *not* exist.

"A middle-level trader at the investment banks making $150,000 per year has no chance at making the big bucks unless he swings for the fences," said Barry. "A trader is retarded if he does not. In fact, I am beating myself up every day that I didn't take more huge bets before I left the bank. There are only three possible outcomes for betting the ranch. One, either your rogue bet loses big money; two, it is 'discovered' by the risk management police before you can close it, or, three, you make big money. In the event of either one or two, you will probably get fired. But in this business, it takes about sixty seconds to find another job. The pursuing bank may even think they are poaching you from one of their competitors, so you might even get a bump in salary. If the bet pays off, sure, your boss will be ticked off that you took a rogue trade but his bonus will be a lot fatter, too—probably fat enough to overlook it. To him, you're a hero. You get a slap on the wrist, a wink, and you're ready for your next swing."

Barrel of Monkeys

It is not all serious money-making on the trading floor. The relationships forged there can be quite strong because of the camaraderie.[7] The team mentality can be as strong as it is in sports. Thick skin is essential, because the bathroom jokes and raging tempers and high stress can make for conversation that would make even Alec Baldwin blush. But you love these guys. They are like brothers.

One of the fun distractions at one of the funds at which I traded was playing video games. Video games had become very competitive through group play, run on the company network. It was as addictive as crack. There was one game

---

7. Less so at hedge funds because they are rigorously aligned by profit center and there is a far less congenial atmosphere than at, say, the investment banks.

that negatively affected the productivity of our office for over a year. Nothing got done. It was called *Half-Life*. The enterprising technology team installed a version on the computer at every trading desk. Hours upon hours of each day were wasted by the traders immersing themselves in this reality game at the peril of their own profits and losses. Who cares if the markets are tumbling? I just made a great kill using my Gauss gun.[8]

During that time such diversions were infectious all across the Street. A trader who used to work at Citigroup told me, "Nelson Mandela was doing a tour of the New York financial industry and he was scheduled to visit us. By the time he reached the trading floor, he came upon a room of flailing, undulating, screaming, and laughing traders, disemboweling and killing each other on their screens in a massive game of *Doom*. No one even looked up as the venerable South African toured the aisles. Nobody wanted to mess up his score by missing an on-screen kill. It was like the substitute teacher showing up to the classroom to find utter mayhem. I will never forget the befuddled look on Mandela's face. He could not reconcile that this was how famed American traders practiced their profession."

If It Walks Like a Duck and Quacks Like a Duck . . .

I have made many references throughout the book to conducting your own research and trusting your instincts. If a trade does not seem reasonable, it probably isn't. If a position appears to be a risky proposition, it probably is. If rigor mortis starts to set in on your great idea, it is probably dead.

Michael, a partner at a major hedge fund, once told me a memorable story about instincts. It was way back in the 1990s,

---

8. Renamed the Tau cannon in later versions of *Half-Life*.

and his firm was helping to issue debt for the much-hyped satellite phone offered by Iridium. This phone, it was widely thought, would change the world. At the time, there was no available worldwide cellular network, so the satellite phone idea was compelling. You would be able to call anyone anywhere at any time. You could call your grandmother from the peaks of the Himalayas or the rural villages of Montenegro.

The question from the very beginning was whether the company would be able to deliver on its promise. The first few attempts to launch a satellite to provide the service were failures. The company nonetheless was flush with cash because it was capitalized through project finance. It had no assets, just a business plan and the satellites. The bonds were very well accepted by the market and immediately traded to 118, or a premium, from their initial offering at par 100. (If the bond is trading at par, its realized return is lower than the coupon, or the interest rate on the bond.)

"Investors were excited to see the phone," Michael told me. "But the company always had a delay or excuse in showing the prototype to investors."

The investors, of course, wanted to see the phone to determine if it would sell. Finally, the company delivered working prototypes to its key institutional investors. At this point, the bonds were still trading at 115.

The phone, as delivered, was as big as a Shaquille O'Neal size twenty-three shoebox. It was big, black, and heavy as hell.

"Who the hell is going to *use* this phone?" Michael asked. "If you are in a war zone and someone is shooting at you, or if you are in the jungles of Africa and a rhinoceros is chasing you, this is the *last* thing you would want to carry. Who would even be able to lug this barbell around and be mobile? The phone also had a huge, 'gi-normous' antenna. Who are you going to hide from? In a war zone, you would be seen easily by snipers or anyone else looking for you. This phone could likely be seen from space. It just didn't make common sense."

Michael told me that to clinch their growing suspicions, he and some other traders turned on the phone on the twenty-fifth floor of a Manhattan office tower to call home and brag to their friends and family that they had the latest telecom technology. The phone simply would not work. They called the company, and the company informed them that in some densely built-up areas the phone wouldn't work because it could not get a direct connect to the satellite.

Michael thought to himself that if it would not work in Manhattan, it certainly would not work in the mountainous Himalayas, as advertised. Plus, the phone was obscenely expensive. If it didn't work properly, it was just an expensive paperweight. Using common sense despite the hype, Michael turned around and sold absolutely every bond he had and eventually started selling them short.

All of his colleagues—also participants in the transaction—thought he had lost his mind. It was the equivalent of shorting Google on the day of its IPO. Eventually, however, based on failed expectations, the bonds fell from 118 to 70 cents on the dollar. There was so much debt in the company and so little delivered that the game was finally up, as others got wise to what was going on. Even when the market price was 70, Michael was selling as much as he could, in blocks, at 65, a significant discount. It was an abject disaster for the company and a very profitable windfall for the short sellers.

According to Michael, the best traders buy themes. "Not every trade is going to be clear as a result of number crunching. Sometimes the obvious is staring you in the face. Great trades are always a combination of the mathematical data and the common-sense filter. Yes, you have to crunch numbers as the final vetting of an idea, but you have to do the head check of 'does this make sense' and look at it fundamentally. Every trade is not just EBITDA[9] and ripping apart annual reports; it also should be based on common sense."

Conclusion

That's what this book has been about: using common sense, free resources, patience, and a little creativity to construct hedged, risk-controlled, sustainable strategies in your own portfolio. Based on the instruments now available to the average trader, you are virtually unlimited in ways to express your ideas. Be circumspect about secular trends that can benefit your portfolio and aware of defensive positions or hedges that can protect it when things change—and they always do. The most important step is adopting the mind-set that a hedge is your objective.

I hope I have convinced you that the big players are not doing anything you cannot. Discipline and consistency would be great attributes to have for any endeavor, but they have particular importance in developing a trading strategy. Also challenging will be to absorb the free information that is all around you and to turn that data into actionable information from which to profit. For the most part, you do not have to read anything more difficult than the headlines of any national or international newspaper.

Once trading, have the courage to change and the patience to let your ideas develop. Close your ears to the talking heads, because they are peddling old ideas. Over time, you will see yourself developing into an opinionated authority (probably to the great chagrin of your spouse).

The downfall of traders is almost always their lack of risk

---

9. Earnings before interest, tax, depreciation, and amortization.

control. Know yourself and your wallet, and stick to the strategy that fits with your expectation of return and your tolerance for loss. One great and simple risk tool is diversification. Make sure you have plenty of ideas in your portfolio. Seek a balance for the number of positions as well as sectors. A portfolio full of one hundred gold or energy stocks is not diversified.

Last, have fun. My mother and father called me over the weekend, beaming about the adjustments they made to their investments. They faxed me everything so that I could render my own opinion. After taking a look at it, I realized that there was absolutely nothing I could add or say that would have made their portfolio better for their age. It was both a moment of pride, and abject depression. Could it really be *that* easy?

ACKNOWLEDGMENTS

I would like to acknowledge the encouragement and patience of my agent, Al Zuckerman. Without his guidance and good humor this work would never have happened.

I would like to thank Stephen Leeb, editor of *The Complete Investor*, for encouraging me to write a book and, in particular, for deftly redirecting my attention back to the "old-school" fundamentals. Our discussions have truly been a gift.

I would like to thank Kenneth Wapner for diligently and enthusiastically providing feedback, helping to improve my work and, most important, keeping me to a schedule.

I would like to give my deep gratitude for all of the crazy characters I have met along the way who made these stories possible to tell.

I have had a great experience with Grand Central Publishing. Thanks to Rick Wolff for helping me to find a personal voice on a topic of relative complexity. Thanks to Karen Andrews for rendering bedfellows of "law" and "humor." And many thanks to the fine editorial team at Business Plus, including Bob Castillo and Tracy Martin.

Last, I would like to thank Gabrijela for putting up with me while I wrote this book in my "spare time." Thank you!

INDEX